# NOTES ON INDIA.

# NOTES
ON THE
# NORTH-WESTERN PROVINCES
OF
# INDIA.

BY

**CHARLES RAIKES**

GYAN

*Published by*

GYAN

Gyan Publishing House
5, Ansari Road
Daryaganj, New Delhi-110002
Phone: 011-47034999, 9811692060
E-mail: books@gyanbooks.com

*Distribution Network*
gyanbooks.com
India, USA, Canada, UK, Australia, France



ISBN: 978-81-212-8264-2 (PB)
First Published, 1852

2nd Impression 2023

*Printed at:* Gyan Press, Delhi.



**NOTES ON THE NORTH-WESTERN PROVINCES OF INDIA**
Author: CHARLES RAIKES

# NOTES ON INDIA.

# NOTES

ON THE

# NORTH-WESTERN PROVINCES

OF

# INDIA.

---

By CHARLES RAIKES,

MAGISTRATE AND COLLECTOR OF MYNPOORIE.

---

Dedicated to the Members of the Civil Service in India.

LONDON:

CHAPMAN AND HALL, 193 PICCADILLY.

MDCCCLII.

# INTRODUCTION.

The Notes on the North-Western Provinces of India, which are now offered to the English reader, were written originally for the "Benares Magazine," and have, with the exception of the last paper, appeared in late numbers of that periodical. The humble attempt of the writer is to describe, in a popular manner, the working of our civil administration in that part of India to which he is attached by the ties of duty and long service. He is induced to offer his observations to a larger circle than is embraced by the "Benares Magazine"* by the following considerations. At the present moment, when the affairs of India engage the public attention, it is believed that a

* This periodical, able and deserving though it be, circulates as yet only amongst a small phase of English readers in India, and is scarcely known in England.

few simple details of the working of our Police and Revenue systems, though given by one who has better means of observing than talents for recording his observations, may be not unacceptable to the general reader. And if that increasing and important class of our public men in England, who take an intelligent interest in British India, should find here little that is new to them, there are still hundreds, nay, thousands, who would gladly see a popular description of the every-day duties which occupy their sons or brothers in the Indian Civil Service.

To that service the writer belongs. No one knows better than he does how dry are the subjects of Indian police practice or revenue science (for a science it is); but it is this very reason which has induced him to attempt, in some poor degree, to attract attention to questions so important to millions of our fellow-subjects. If, by his imperfect endeavour to sketch the condition of the people as affected by the policy of their English masters, he has added but one stone to the monument of Christian civilisation, which so many abler hands are striving to rear in India, his labour will not have been in vain.

Such being the scope of the writer, a few words more may be excused as to the detail of his book.

The first place has been given to the note on "Female Infanticide," because that paper has been honoured by the approbation of the Lieutenant-governor of Agra, to whom it was originally inscribed, and has been distributed by that distinguished statesman to the magistrates and other public servants in the Upper Provinces.

The next four numbers of the Notes, from two to five inclusive, belong to the subject of Landed Tenures in the North-Western Provinces. No. II. sketches the Rise and Progress of our Revenue System. No. III. sketches the Character of the Rajpoot Agriculturist, and the Condition of the Landed Proprietors under British rule.

No. IV. continues the subject of No. III., and proceeds to consider the case of the Non-proprietary Cultivating Classes.

No. V. contains the Domestic History of a Rajpoot Family, as affected by the proceedings of a Magistrate and Collector.

Nos. VI. to VIII. present a sketch of the duties of a Magistrate in the North-Western

Provinces. These "Notes on the Police" were written to form a *pendant* to the "Notes on Landed Tenures," given in Nos. II. to V. The last of the Police Notes has not yet appeared in print in India.

The extracts given in Nos. V., VI., and VII., as from the Note-book of a Magistrate and Collector, describe scenes through which the writer has himself passed—in short, facts, not fancies; as, indeed, the reader may conclude from the ordinary nature of many of the circumstances related.

# I.

## FEMALE INFANTICIDE IN THE DOAB.*

It was our national enemy who dubbed the English "a nation of shopkeepers." There was more of wit than of truth in the sentence. For if, in matters of mere traffic and commerce, the English mind be guarded and cautious, it is in other moral or social relations remarkable for frank unsuspecting confidence. The hearts of our countrymen are prone to belief; we speak, not only of their deep natural faith in the realities of the unseen world, but we say, also, that Englishmen in general walk this every-day life with believing hearts.

One special faith there is, deep in the mind of England, which our present subject has suggested to us, and that is, the faith in female virtue. The Englishman, and, thank Heaven, with good reason, is a believer in the purity of the female sex: to his mind (we speak of all except the professed liber-

* Land between two rivers. In Hindostan the vast and fertile tract situated between the Ganges and Jumna is known as "The Doạb."

tine) the innocence of girlhood is a reality, whilst he regards with equal respect the vow of the matron or the veil of the widow. And what individuals believe, the common voice of the nation ratifies. As a people, we venerate the quiet charities of domestic life. In late years, when almost every European dynasty seemed to shake, the throne of England has needed no surer bulwark than that which the love of a nation could supply. To a monarch who, to the dignity of a queen, added the graces of a wife and a mother, who had shown herself in all these relations so faithful, what honest English heart could be faithless? How immense the effect upon our national character of this one article of our fireside religion, can best be told by those who, in less favoured societies, have tried to lead or raise the human mind.

In India we are reminded, at every turn, how hard it is to affect the domestic morals of a nation which believes not in female honour and virtue. No man is more impatient of female disgrace than your Rajpoot or Brahmin, but no man is more incredulous of female fidelity. Girlhood he watches with doubt, married life with jealousy, widowhood —the very word is a reproach.* Men who prophesy thus of their women need not be surprised if their prophecies come true. The woman of India is what the man has made her. But so is woman everywhere: educate her, trust her, woman

* The word *rand*, or widow, is a common term of abuse.

will be virtuous; cramp her mind, pamper and confine her body, show her that she is degraded, and degraded she will be, whether in the seraglio of the East or the salons of Europe.

Reflecting, as one is apt to do, rather bitterly on the degraded condition of the women of India, the thought will arise, how little has England done for her*—how few and feeble the attempts that have been made to raise her position or to defend her rights. Rights of woman! Alas! in India these may be summed up in few words,—to suffer, and to die. The sufferings of the sex have been well touched by a happier pen than ours.

"To the fair of other lands the fate of the "Rajpootnee must appear one of appalling hard-"ship. In each stage of life Death is ready to "claim her—by the poppy at its dawn, by the "flames in riper years; while, the safety of the "interval depending on the uncertainty of war, "at no period is her existence worth a twelve-"month's purchase. The loss of a battle or the "capture of a city is a signal to avoid captivity "and its horrors, which, to the Rajpootnee, are "worse than death."†

The woman of India has suffered deep and

* There are a few bright exceptions to this rule, and lately a very noble attempt to elevate the native female has been made in Calcutta under the auspices of Mr. Drinkwater Bethune, to which we emphatically wish "God speed."

† Tod's "Annals of Rajasthan." The annalist here refers to the Rajpoot practice of sacrificing their women rather than let them fall into an enemy's hands.

long, but she has suffered in silence, and her sufferings have been, at least in appearance, voluntary—with her own hand has she lighted the funeral fires which were to consume her life along with the lifeless body of her husband; and (in some races) with her own hand has she quenched the spark of infant vitality as each girl was born to her. Our earlier settlers in India, intent on commerce and wealth, had little opportunity to notice the wrongs of the women of the country. At a later period they were averse to meddling with the customs of the people, and at home, unless the sufferings of some Begum of rank could be worked up into "political capital," little notice was likely to be taken of the women of India.* Later still, Lord William Bentinck found it no easy matter to fight the battles of the innocent uncomplaining widow, amidst the official apathy or secret opposition of men who should have been the first to assist him.

However, our present affair is not with the wrongs of Indian women in general, but with the peculiar and unnatural crime which, amongst cer-

* The females of India and their wrongs were useful when a grand display in Parliament was wanted to crush a political foe.

Every one has heard of Burke's celebrated orations about the Begums of Lucknow, and, above all, that famous peroration about the virgins of Bengal, and their treatment by "the infernal fiend," Devi Singh, at which Mrs. Sheridan fainted, and the orator himself sunk down to cover his face with his hands, overawed by the figures which his own imagination had conjured up.

tain classes, consigns the female infants to immediate death.

And first, to take a more extended glance.

Infanticide is a world-wide crime. Except the land of our own Saxon forefathers, we can scarce name a country unstained by the blood of its infant children. Men of letters and refinement have equalled the savage and surpassed the brute in this special ferocity. In all continents, in Europe, Asia, Africa, and America, in almost every island from the rocks of Iceland to the reefs of the Pacific, the hand of the parent has been lifted against his child. The usual cause in other countries has been want or luxury; in India, either superstition or pride. Before the time of English domination thousands of hapless children were thrown as votive offerings to the river gods. These sacrifices have been stayed; but still, as we write, hundreds of infant females are being hurried out of the world, victims to the pride of their parents.

Let us examine the source of this particular pride, which has proved so tragical to the Rajpootnee girls. Like other martial and gallant races, the early Rajpoots were not insensible to the claims of chivalry. Their women were free. Instead of being mewed up, as is now their lot, in the female apartments, all reasonable liberty was granted to them. Some privileges of the ladies, indeed, remind us of the best days of Romance, and carry us away to the western world, and to the days of Charlemagne or the Crusades. The distressed Rajpootnee damsel, or the forlorn matron in the hour of danger, would send her jewelled bracelet* to some *preux chevalier*, like Bayard of old, *sans peur et sans reproche*, who thenceforth would serve his mistress to the death, nor ask but one return—that she should accept and wear the proffered guerdon of his loyalty, a bodice of silk or embroidery.† History relates that the Emperor Humaioon, son of Baber, was so inspired with romantic devotion on receiving a bracelet thus sent by the Princess Kurnavati in her distress, that, forgetting the usual phlegm of his nature, he pledged himself at once to her service, "vowing "to obey her behest even if the demand were the "castle of Rinthumbor."‡ The knight thus chosen was styled "*Rakhibund bhai*," the bracelet-bound brother; and on such a connexion the breath of scandal was never known to pass. But, not only might the daughter of a Rajpoot thus choose her liege knight, she might do more,—she had a liberty which our own Anglo-Saxon damsels, unless of royal rank, have seldom tasted. She might choose her own husband, and might herself inform the happy lover on whom her choice had fallen. On a given day the chiefs assembled, and, passing through the gallant line of suitors, the Rajpootnee

* *Rakhi.*

† Mr. Rafter, in his "Savindroog," suggests that the corset was chosen as a proof of affection, because that garment is so close to the heart of the wearer; but we are inclined to believe, that it was selected to denote a pure and fraternal gift, it being the custom for brothers to give presents of dress to their married sisters.

‡ Tod's "Annals," quoted by the author of "Savindroog."

maiden threw the *mala*, or garland, over the favoured swain. These assemblies broke up sometimes in so much heat, that at last it was found impossible with safety to convene them. To this day, in the mid Doad, as the sun enters the summer solstice, the village youth while away the glowing nights with the chant of "Ala and Oodun." In these and other such romaunts we learn how readily the disappointed suitors flew to arms, and, with all their love turned into hate, pursued the accepted rival. So much noble blood was shed on an occasion of this sort in the warfare between Jyechund and Pirthee Raj, that from that day no *mala* has been thrown. The Rajpoot tribes, convulsed by internal dissensions, and hardened by frequent warfare, forgot their old chivalrous ways. The gentler sex, who had caused the mischief, were the first to suffer, and their liberty was changed into thraldom. When they could no longer woo or be wooed by fair means, they must be won at all events, and the sword became the arbiter of their lot. The stronger of the Rajpoots began to carry off, by force of arms or by stratagem, the marriageable women of other cognate tribes. This practice gave new life to the old Hindoo superstition* of the *inferior* position of the father-in-law. The son-in-law became, more than ever, the social superior of his father-in-law. If the wife were

* "The point of honour is carried so far, that it is reckoned disgraceful to receive any assistance in after-life from a son-in-law or brother-in-law." — ELPHINSTONE's *India*, vol. i. p. 358.

henceforth a slave, the wife's father need expect but little courtesy or consideration. A Rajpoot of the present day is subject to his son-in-law hand and foot, can refuse him nothing, and, without disgrace, cannot accept so much as a meal at his hands.

There is a tradition prevalent in the Doab, that a Chohan Thakoor, being sorely pressed by his son-in-law, and smarting under the sense of disgrace which his mere position as the father of a married daughter seemed to entail upon him, called together his sons, and bound them by an oath to save his family from future contempt by destroying every female child that might be born to them. Hence, as some say, the origin of female infanticide amongst the Chohan Rajpoots, men in other respects the noblest of a not ignoble race.* But there have been other and more subtle influences at work. At the very root of the evil stands this principle,—the Hindoo disbelieves the purity of the sex; a daughter arrived at puberty *must*, he thinks, be married or be disgraced. When he seeks a husband for her it *must* be in his own caste, but it *must* also be in a subdivision† of that caste; higher, if possible, but at all events differing from his own. To intermarry in one's own subdivision is impossible; such an union would be set down as incestuous. Disgrace is attached to marriages with men of inferior relative rank.

* Tod assigns the first place to the "Chohan" as warriors amongst the thirty-six royal races of Rajpoots.

† "Kool," or "Goth."

"The owner of a hyde of land, whether Seesodea, "Rahtore, or Chohan, would scorn the hand of a "Jareja princess."* What, then, is a Rajpoot father to do with his marriageable daughters? He must, it is clear, seek a husband for them in a rank equal to his own, or in a higher rank. But if his own subdivision be high, if he be a Chohan or a Rahtore, he will not easily find such a son-in-law; or if he do find him, will have to pay high in hard coin for blood and rank. And this is why a Rajpoot mourns when a daughter is born to him, and rejoices when he has a son. The one brings disgrace, anxiety, or at the least heavy expense upon his house; the other increases his wealth and his dignity.

So far, then, we have attempted to trace the domestic position of the Rajpoot girls. This position is a false one. So, it may be said, is that of thousands of their sisters in Europe, who suffer from the prevailing scarcity of husbands. But, in the western world, we have long had convents to receive the unmarried women, and, what is better, we have no false private code of morals ruling, as in India, that celibacy is a disgrace. Hundreds of our best and most useful persons are unmarried women. The state which Christianity has sanctified, heathenism has more than debased; it has annihilated. There is no such element in Indian society as that which the adult unmarried female

* Tod's "Annals."

so gracefully supplies in Europe. A woman in India must marry, or she must cease to be. The conventional rules, then, of society, in which the Rajpoot for some centuries past has found himself, left him but this option,—to give up his pride or his daughters.

On a former occasion* we have sketched the Rajpoot character; we then described him as exceedingly proud and only moderately humane: so, when the question came whether he should part with his humanity or his pride, the evil part of his nature gained the victory. We will not call it an easy victory; they who know the Rajpoot best are aware of his moody sufferings,† of the discontent and discomfort of his soul when he condemns his infant girls to death: but still he has shown little hesitation as to the course he should pursue. The girls of the highest Rajpoot clans have, since the days of Pirthee Raj, been sacrificed, hundreds of families sparing not one female. The hiatus thus caused has been filled up by the daughters of the humbler tribes, and the men of the humblest tribes have often been sore pushed to find a wife at all. When man sets himself up against his Maker, and dares thus habitually to mar His handiwork, what

* See "Notes on the Landed Tenures," Benares Magazine for October 1850.

† It is well known at Mynpoorie that the late Rajah Duleer Singh, when a female infant was made away with in his fort, used to be restless and unhappy, giving away money, a horse, or an elephant to the Brahmins, as though to expiate the crime.

can be expected but vexation and disappointment? And thus we see how the cruel absurd pride of these Rajpoots has ended.

We find a body of men endowed alike with many noble qualities, and all of the same caste. But in this caste there are subdivisions, some of which the voice of custom has pronounced to be high and some low. The high cannot get husbands of sufficient rank for their daughters,—so they kill them; the low being in the mean time obliged to go without wives at all. Where, might we ask, is the vaunted Reason of man when Pride is allowed to shut the light of God from the soul?

But we desist; the subject before us requiring, as old Hooker would say, "not railing, but reasons." The question occurs, Cannot the mind of the European, backed by his power (a power greater than Eastern nation or emperor ever saw), cannot the European with all his vantage ground put down such a miserable practice as this of murdering little children? This question is not to be answered at once, for the evil to be mastered is not in men's bodies only, but in their souls; not only in their acts, but in their motives. A crime, which nips the budding life fresh from the hand of God, seems left for God to punish. Man has not time nor place to step in. The life of a new-born child, we all know, at the best hangs on a single thread. To snap this, any treatment less tender than the caress which even the beast of the forest bestows upon her young, will suffice.

The mere neglect of the ordinary precautions of

the lying-in room, the mere refusal of the mother to perform her first maternal duties, a bowl of water, a rough touch—anything, in short, is enough.* The magistrate can hardly punish men for a want of solicitude about their young; yet without solicitude the young will be lost. So it is only to the very superficial observer, to the very ignorant disciple of the "*sic volo, sic jubeo*" school, that it will appear

* A native has described the manner in which female infants are destroyed in the following words:—

"Milk, which is designed by nature to form the food of the new-born babe, is the substance used for the cruel purpose here referred to. In a vessel full of this nourishing liquid, the stony-hearted parents, or their female attendants, plunge the female infants as soon as they come into existence, and they are made to struggle in it till the vital principle is extinguished in them. Opium is not unfrequently made the instrument through which these Rajpoots perpetrate the horrifying deed. The manner of doing it is thus related:—The mother applies it to the nipples of her breast, and it is insensibly imbibed with the milk by the infant, and has the effect of extinguishing its life. A Rajpoot, who is in my service, told me, when I asked him for some information upon this topic, that his countrymen stick a bit of the drug to the roofs of their infants' mouths, and allow them to remain in this dangerous position for a minute or two, during which the heat of the mouth melts the drug, and it is taken into their system, and hurries them into eternity. The extinction of life is sometimes effected by means of suffocation, the umbilical cord and secundines being placed on the nose and mouth of infants to check respiration. He further added, that his father had made away with the lives of his three sisters in this manner." —*Prize Essay on Female Infanticide*, by Cooverjee Rustomjee Mody, Bombay, 1849. In this work are collected a number of tenets from the Purānas, showing how opposed is the practice of child-murder to the religious tenets of the Hindoos.

an easy thing to put down such a crime as this.* Young and ardent men advocate a sort of physical-force system; older and more experienced heads are all for moral suasion and expostulation. A *via media* between the extremes of inquisitorial severity and mere protestation is, we believe, the right course. On the whole, we think that in our own provinces the delicacy shown to the feelings of a race, who show so little common humanity themselves, has been carried quite far enough; and we proceed to give our reasons for advocating a little more general and direct supervision of the Rajpoots of the N. W. Provinces than has yet been considered necessary. Before doing so we may just remark, that we do not blame the magistrates of Upper India, who, although they have put down almost all open violent crime, have not as yet been able to cope with this secret wickedness. It is only lately that much attention has been directed to statistical inquiry, and, without such inquiry,

* Under the old Roman law infanticide was winked at, and the crime was easily put down when it was made by Valentinian and his colleagues (by including such murders in the Cornelian law) a capital offence to expose a child. In India, a law (XXI. 1795) similar to that of the Roman Emperor was promulgated in the end of the last century, but with very different effect; that is to say, with scarcely any effect at all upon the cruel habits of the people. A sufficient reason for this may, perhaps, be found in the different domestic habits of the people. A Roman lived comparatively *in public*, and could only make away with his child by sending it to a distant forest or other exposed place. A Rajpoot lives *in private*, with high walls enclosing a considerable area; and in his domestic privacy the crime of infanticide can be practised with little risk of detection.

the disproportion between male and female infants is not observed. The crime of infanticide, for the obvious reasons which we have already given, is not easily brought home to any particular person. The death of an adult can only be compassed by force or stratagem, and will probably create inquiry and suspicion; the mere putting a new-born infant out of the way is a much simpler matter, and can generally be accomplished without risk or trouble. And when the very strongest suspicions have seemed to warrant a committal of the parents to take their trial at the Sessions Court, it has been found impossible to obtain a conviction.*

We only remember the names of two men who have been known at all to the public for their exertions to put down female infanticide north of the Caramnasa. Jonathan Duncan early called atten-

* The following extract from a calendar of prisoners committed by a magistrate in 1849, gives an outline of a case in which there was not the slightest doubt of the guilt of the parents, but, nevertheless, no conviction could be got at the sessions. The judge in this case was heard to observe, that he did not doubt the guilt of the accused, but that, supposing him to have been innocent, he might equally have run away and borrowed a child. In short, it is almost impossible to prove the actual murder in such cases.

" It is customary in this district, with the object of checking " Female Infanticide, to register the births and deaths of female " infants born in Chohan Thakoor families. On the 26th Sep- " tember, 1848, the birth of a female child in the house of Gun- " durrup Singh of Kirpuree, was reported at the Kotwallie. On " the 13th November, it was reported that the child was ill—a " burkundauze was sent to see her, and returning stated that " the child was well. It was subsequently proved that, on the

tion to the crime in the Benares Province; but, beyond declaring the criminality of the act, we are not aware that he put into execution any measures for its prevention. We believe he recommended that the Rajpootnee girls should have dowers paid them by Government. The Court of Directors negatived this proposal, and no wonder, lest good men who killed no daughters and got no dowers might be tempted to imitate the Rajpoots' example.

At a later period, as we learn from an interesting article in the "Calcutta Review,"* Mr. R. Montgomery, when magistrate of Allahabad, set earnestly to work to put down infanticide amongst some of the Rajpoots. His measures bear the practical stamp which has marked all the proceedings of this distinguished public officer. "In "the first place," says he, "I appointed a chu-

"occasion of the visit of the burkundauze, a neighbour's child "was shown. There was reason to suspect that Gundurrup "Singh, and Mussummutt Bukt Kenwur his wife, had destroyed "their child. They had left their village; but in January were "brought in, and their case investigated. There were very "strong grounds for suspicion, but not enough to justify a "commitment till later, when intelligence was received from "Shajehanpore that these persons had been over to a village in "that district to borrow a child, with the object of personating "an infant which it was supposed they had destroyed. This "transaction being fully proved, and the bones of an infant "being dug up in Gundurrup Sing's out-house, for which he "could give no account, he and his wife were committed to "take their trial for murder, and Bhubootee Singh as accessory "after the fact."

* "Calcutta Review," No. 2, on Female Infanticide.

"prassee to reside in each village, whose sole duty "it was to report the birth of a female child in the "families of any of the above classes of Rajputs. "I also bound the gorait, chowkidar, and mid-"wives, under a heavy penalty, to report separ-"ately each birth at the thannah, the four thus "acting as a check on each other. I directed "the thanadar, on the death of any female infant "being reported, to hold an inquest on the body, "and afterwards to transmit it to the civil surgeon "for examination. I associated the tehsildar with "the thanadar, in order to ensure a more efficient "superintendence; I promised them both hand-"some rewards if I should be hereafter satisfied "that they, by their joint efforts, had put a stop to "the horrible practice."

"I am happy to state, that, as far as I am able "to judge, the method I have pursued has been "attended with perfect success. It is only two "months since the plan came into operation, and "of four female infants that have since been born, "three are alive, and one dead."—*Report by the Magistrate of Allahabad in* 1841.

We do not consider that the amount of *espionage* enforced by Mr. Montgomery is desirable; and though such a system might be safely and efficiently worked by the able hand of the present Commissioner of Lahore, we are not disposed to see our magistrates throughout the provinces enforcing so close an inquisition. We have already said there is a *via media*, which neither sets a premium on crime like Mr. Duncan's dowry scheme, nor yet presses so heavily on the Rajpoot pride as Mr. Montgomery's system.

We must recollect what the Rajpoot once was in better days. No Norman knight at the court of Rouen, or in the days of Tancred, could show more delicate devotion to the gentle sex than did the early princes of Rajpootana. This spirit is quenched; their martial habits are, under our system, necessarily decaying. We must take heed lest we rob them of what alone is left them,—their self-respect. In devising measures for putting down female infanticide amongst the Rajpoots, the advice of men of other castes cannot be trusted. Hindoo and Mahometan would alike rejoice to ride rough-shod over the pride of the Thakoor, and jealousy easily puts on the cloak of virtuous indignation: yet, regard as we may their feelings, something may be done, and perhaps something more than has yet been done in general, to let the Rajpoot *feel* that the eye of the Anglo-Saxon is upon him, and that his sins shall some day find him out.

Happily we are not left here to mere speculation. The experiment of a modified and regulated supervision *has been tried*, during the last six years, over a considerable tract of country, in the head-quarters of one of the chief Rajpoot tribes, and with no small success.

Many of our readers will recollect the famine of 1838, (none, indeed, who were then in the N. W. Provinces will ever forget it,) when mothers sold their children for a morsel of bread, when the rage of hunger obliterated even the distinctions of caste, and the Brahmin might be seen devouring the leavings of the Dhom.* Nowhere did hunger and disease press heavier than in the plains of the mid Doab. Whole villages were depopulated, and every effort of public or private benevolence failed to meet the wants of a starving population. The Government did much to relieve the sufferers at the time, but a merely temporary assistance was not sufficient, and it became necessary to lower the revenue demand in many villages. Mr. Unwin, then Collector of Mynpoorie, was in 1842 engaged in fixing the amount of this revision, and his camp was pitched in the midst of the villages of the Chohan Rajpoots. In the course of his proceedings it was found desirable to ascertain how far the population had been affected by the famine, and with this object Mr. Unwin determined to take ten villages in each pergunneh, and selecting one house in each of these villages, to count in person every head in it. "In so doing," we use his own words, "I observed what previous in-"formation led me to expect, that no single "Chohanee (female Chohan), young or old, was "forthcoming.† I remarked this to the Zemindars

* The lowest caste.

† The wives were, of course, not Chohanee, as Chohan cannot wed with Chohanee. The higher Chohan usually seeks alliances for his daughters (if they are preserved alive) with the Kuchwaee, Budhoreea, Bughela, Rathore; and the humbler Chohan will take a female from the Pureehar of Bundelcund and the Jadhen

"and people themselves, who, of course, were in "numbers all about me on these occasions, and "told them I knew the cause, and should look "after them in future."

Mr. Unwin acted with zeal and discretion, and above all things (in India) with *promptitude.* At once and on his own responsibility he established a system of watchful inspection, which was thus described by the officiating magistrate of Mynpoorie (in 1848), in reply to a call for information from the Court of Directors:—*

"In Chohan villages the watchmen are ordered to give in-"formation of the birth of a female child forthwith at the police "station. A burkundauze goes to the house and sees the child, "the thanadar informs the magistrate, upon which an order is "passed, that after one month the health of the new-born child "should be reported. The watchmen are further bound to give "information if any illness attack the child, when a superior "police-officer (either thanadar, jemadar, or mohurrir), at once "goes to the village, sees the child, and sends a report to the "magistrate. In suspicious cases the body of the child is sent "for and submitted to the Civil Surgeon."

---

of Kurowlie, near Jyepoor. Beyond this we do not think they often go,—or, to use their own phraseology, *lower* than this. The chief Chohan families in the mid Doab are at Mynpoorie, Rujore, Etah, Ekah, Chukurnuggur, and Purtabneir. The Budhoreea Goth is originally the same as the Chohan, but intermarriage is now allowed between the two tribes.

* Mr. Unwin received cordial assistance from Mr. Robert Thornhill, at that time Joint-Magistrate of Mynpoorie, whose attention, as well as that of every officer who has since been in the district, has been constantly given to watch the working of Mr. Unwin's scheme.

The effect of Mr. Unwin's measures was soon felt in the district. Amongst other incidents we may quote the following, as partaking of that almost grotesque character which in these matter-of-fact days seems peculiar to India. The Government had watched Mr. Unwin's proceedings with approbation, and took an early opportunity to notify in a public manner the interest which was felt in the success of his measures.

There is at Mynpoorie an old fortress, which looks far over the valley of the Eesun river. This has been for centuries the stronghold of the Rajahs of Mynpoorie, Chohans whose ancient blood, descending from the great Pirthee Raj and the regal stem of Neem-rana, represents *la crême de la crême* of Rajpoot aristocracy. Here when a son, a nephew, a grandson, was born to the reigning chief, the event was announced to the neighbouring city by the loud discharge of wall-pieces and matchlocks; but centuries had passed away, and no infant daughter had been known to smile within those walls.

In 1845, however, thanks to the vigilance of Mr. Unwin, a little grand-daughter was preserved by the Rajah of that day. The fact was duly notified to the Government, and a letter of congratulation and a dress of honour were at once despatched from head-quarters to the Rajah.

We have called this incident, the giving a robe of honour to a man because he did not destroy his grand-daughter, a *grotesque* one; but it is very far from being a ridiculous incident. When the people see that the highest authorities in the land take an interest in their social or domestic reforms, those reforms receive an impetus which no lesser influences can give them. The very next year after the investiture of the Rajah, the number of female infants preserved in the district was *trebled !* Fifty-seven had been saved in 1845 ; in 1846, one hundred and eighty were preserved ; and the number has gone on steadily increasing ever since. This is the best answer to those who would sneer at the *paternal* style of Government, and who would advocate mere red-tape, law, and bayonets for the people of India.

Influence is everything in Hindostan. Indeed in all countries good government, like true religion, depends upon influences and motives quite as much as upon mere rules and restrictions. In England, influence does *much ;* in India, we repeat, it does *all.* To go against the *law* is nothing to the native of India, but he rarely consents to go against the *magistrate.* When a government of mere law comes in, when *codes* instead of *men* are to rule India, the sooner the English are off to their ships the better. Let us see what local influence, supported by the influence of the Government, but scarcely assisted by legal sanction, has done for the suppression of female infanticide in Mynpoorie. In 1843, not a single female Chohan infant was to be found in the district ; at the present moment there are fourteen hundred girls living, between the ages of one and six. We subjoin an extract from the official Registers, from 1844 to 1850 inclusive. The girls born during the year, and still alive at the end of the year, are only entered :—

| Name of Thannah. | 1844 | 1845 | 1846 | 1847 | 1848 | 1849 | 1850 | Total. | Girls of 6 years and under, living in May 1851. |
|---|---|---|---|---|---|---|---|---|---|
| Koorowlie | 7 | 2 | 19 | 1 | 15 | 15 | 24 | 83 | 119 |
| Shekoabad | 9 | 8 | 2 | 6 | 13 | 15 | 22 | 75 | 80 |
| Bhowgong | 5 | 4 | 3 | 8 | 8 | 7 | 10 | 45 | 60 |
| Koosmurra | 11 | 3 | 3 | 2 | 5 | 3 | 17 | 44 | 55 |
| Kurhul ... | 1 | 7 | 5 | 4 | 9 | 7 | 10 | 43 | 33 |
| Sumao ... | 58 | 8 | 35 | 44 | 53 | 46 | 43 | 287 | 145 |
| Mynpoorie | 28 | 10 | 57 | 57 | 77 | 97 | 108 | 434 | 353 |
| Ghurour ... | 15 | 9 | 21 | 41 | 36 | 61 | 57 | 240 | 234 |
| Sirsa-gunge | 0 | 2 | 2 | 2 | 1 | 0 | 1 | 8 | 8 |
| Kyleyee ... | 0 | 4 | 25 | 43 | 29 | 38 | 43 | 182 | 140 |
| Phurrah ... | 0 | 0 | 8 | 1 | 15 | 13 | 13 | 50 | 38 |
| Total ... | 134 | 57 | 180 | 209 | 261 | 302 | 348 | 1491 | 1263 |

To check these results, a census of the entire Chohan population of the district, of six years old and under, has been made in the present year. The plan adopted was, first to call upon the village accountants to report the numbers of boys and girls, up to the age of six, living in their respective villages. These returns were then tested as closely as possible by other independent officials, and, as the result of that examination, the number of females was reduced eleven per cent. The return thus corrected is as follows, and is given for pergunnehs, not for the thannahs, noted in the former table :—

| Names of Pergunnehs. | Boys 6 years and under. | Girls 6 years and under. | REMARKS. |
|---|---|---|---|
| Ghurour ... ... ... | 297 | 194 | The distribution of the 1263 girls into their respective thannahs will be found in the last column of the preceding table.* |
| Souj ... ... ... ... | 376 | 219 | |
| Kurhul ... ... ... | 52 | 33 | |
| Koorowlie ... .. ... | 33 | 17 | |
| Mustúfabad and Shekoabad ... ... | 474 | 299 | |
| Kishnee Nubbee Gunge | 261 | 102 | |
| Munchuna ... ... ... | 364 | 246 | |
| Bhowgong ... ... ... | 283 | 150 | |
| Aleepoor Puttee ... ... | 21 | 3 | |
| Total ... | 2161 | 1263 | |

* In 1850, inquiries were made in 66 villages as to the comparative number of children in existence amongst the Chohan Thakoors, the Patuk Aheers (who are suspected of practising female infanticide), and other classes. The boys of six years old or under numbered 2770, the girls 2004.

| | | | |
|---|---|---|---|
| Of these, Chohans have | 614 boys to | 293 girls. |
| Patuk Aheers | 120 ,, | 94 ,, |
| Other Castes | 2036 ,, | 1617 ,, |
| Total .. | 2770 Boys. | 2004 Girls. |

From a census lately taken in the neighbouring district of Etaweh, it appears, that 8253 boys of ten years and under were found to 4589 girls. Yet, in 1849, the births of 479 boys were reported, and as many as 716 girls.

It is notorious all over the world, that it is only in highly-civilized, and probably we might say Christianised societies, that the females who are reared by their parents equal in number the males. In India, where the male child is, owing to the peculiar religious tenets of the people, so much desired, the daughters are never cared for as the sons are, and the number reared even in families who do not practise infanticide is not equal to that of the sons. Still the disproportion amongst the Chohans is so great, that taken alone, even if other proof were wanting, it would go far to prove the prevalence of female infanticide.

We will not weary our readers with more figures. It will suffice to express our conviction that, whereas formerly scarce one female escaped with life, now *at least* one out of two is preserved. The Rajpoot fathers are beginning to take a pride in their little daughters, and often bring them out to make their *salaam* to the English officer as he passes their villages.

The case, then, of the females of the higher Rajpoot castes may be thus summed up. In days long gone by they were treated with respect, and even with gallantry; in later times their lot has been a hard one. At the present day, the head of a Rajpoot household considers that he must find a husband for his daughter, and one of good family. But such a husband is only to be got for money, and the sum required, when added to the other indispensable marriage expenses,* is more than

* We have not said enough, and we could hardly say too much, in reprobation of the extortionate demands made by the *bhats*, and other hangers-on of the Rajpoot families, on the occasion of a wedding. Colonel Tod says on this subject—"Un-" fortunately those who could check nuptial profusion find their " interest in stimulating it, namely, the whole class of *mangtus* " (mendicants), bards, minstrels, jugglers, Brahmins, who as-" semble on these occasions, and pour forth their epithalamia in " praise of the virtue of liberality. The *bardais* are the grand " recorders of fame, and the volume of precedent is always " recurred to, in citing the liberality of former chiefs; while the " dread of their satire (*viserva*, literally *poison*) shuts the eyes " of the chiefs to consequences, and they are only anxious to " maintain the reputation of their ancestors, though fraught with " future ruin.

" 'The Dahirna emptied his coffers' (says Chund, the pole-

most men can afford. Hence the Rajpoot father has been driven to the alternative of sacrificing his family pride or his daughters. He has preferred sin to what he considers shame, and has carried his prejudices so far, that in certain parts of the country the female children have all been systematically destroyed. But it appears that a regulated system of espionage and supervision, supported by the influence of the Government and of the local authorities, has been found effectual to the putting down of this crime to a considerable extent.

The question remains, and a very interesting question it is, What more can be done? If half of the females have been saved, let us set to work to preserve the remainder. In the first place, it might be well to extend the Mynpoorie system of supervision to all districts in which the infant females

"star of the Rajpoots) 'on the marriage of his daughter with "Pirthiráj; but he filled them with the praises of mankind.' "The same bard retails every article of these *daejas* or dowers, "which thus becomes precedents for future ages; and the "'*lac passao*' then established for the chief *bardai* has become a model to posterity. Even now the Rana of Oodipoor, "in his season of poverty, at the recent marriage of his daughters, bestowed the gift of a lac on the chief bard; though "the articles of gold, horses, clothes, &c. were included in the "estimate, and at an undue valuation, which rendered the gift "not quite so precious as in the days of the Chohan. Were bonds "taken from all the feudal chiefs, and a penal clause inserted "of forfeiture of their fief by all who exceeded a fixed nuptial "expenditure, the axe would be laid to the root, the evil would "be checked, and the heart of many a mother" (and we may add, father) "be gladdened, by preserving at once the point of "honour and their child."—TOD's *Annals of Rajasthan*.

are destroyed, and to every tribe suspected of female infanticide. Another plan remains to be tried, which may complete a reform already so well begun. Though nothing new, it has not yet been tried on a large scale in our Provinces.* We allude to the regulating by authority the amount of dowers.

* From Mynpoorie the system of supervision extended, about 1847, to the neighbouring district, and we observe that this experiment was made by Mr. E. H. C. Monckton, when officiating as Magistrate of Etaweh in 1849. He called upon the heads of the Thakoor families to execute engagements in punchayet, for the putting down female infanticide. Here is a specimen of the papers given in on the occasion :—

"We Peetum Singh, Bisal Singh, Bhoop Singh, Hoolass "Singh, &c., who have been summoned to be admonished not "to commit female infanticide, beg to state that we do not "murder our female children; but, as matter of precaution, we "have now settled amongst ourselves by arbitration that, if any "of our brethren be in indigent circumstances, and have not the "means of defraying the marriage expenses, we will assist him "to do so. To murder female infants is held in detestation "by us. The opinion prevalent, that we consider it an abuse to "be called father-in-law, is false: we do not think it to be so, "nor do we take offence at it. Should any one among us be guilty "of such an act, we will excommunicate him, and he will render "himself liable to punishment by the ruling power, and to the "wrath of the Day of Judgment. If at any time it should "appear to the authorities that any one among us has com- "mitted infanticide, we will expel him from our society, and "deliver over his children to become the property of the Go- "vernment. If to our knowledge any of our brotherhood should "be guilty of the crime of infanticide, we will banish him from "our society, and report the circumstance to authority.

"With reference to the report that we do not allow the female "children to take nourishment from the mother's breast, we beg "to state that it is false; should any one do so, he will be

No one can converse much with the Rajpoots themselves on this matter without being asked, Why does not the English Government forbid the ex-

" liable to the same punishment as we have resolved upon for " those who may commit infanticide. As to the statement that " when a pregnant woman draws near her time we send her over " to the Murhattah territories, with a view to destroy the infant's " life if a girl, and after doing so the mother is recalled; we beg " to say, that although this is not the fact, we have determined " as a prudent measure, that if any one among our class should " send over his pregnant wife to the Murhattah territories with " the intention of destroying the child if a girl, that we will ex- " communicate him.

" In regard to the marriage of girls we have come to these " resolutions, viz. that as it is not justifiable for the father of " the boy to cause the father of the girl to enter into such con- " ditions as to marriage settlement as suit his wishes, only before " closing the nuptial contract (because, if the girl's father be " poor, the marriage cannot take place, and must be necessarily " put off), we therefore propose that the headmen of the village " should arrange the dower according to the circumstances in " life of the girl's father, and to this arrangement he must con- " sent; and that whenever the girl's father receives a proposal " from the boy's father, he should immediately declare that he " is willing to abide by the decision of the arbitrators or head- " men *as to amount* of dower."

In reporting to the Government Mr. Monckton's proceedings, the Commissioner of Agra, Mr. Robinson, who had long watched the measures adopted in the Mynpoorie and Etaweh districts for putting down child murder, writes:—

" His honour is well aware that the main incentive to the " practice is the enormous expenses that are by custom thrown " on the parents when a daughter is married, and I really be- " lieve that a law, protecting the people from these expenses, " and, under the cloak of the power of Government, saving the " disgrace that attaches to refusing to incur those expenses, " would be gladly received by the people."

action of dowers? Why is not security taken from our chiefs to prevent the fixing of dowers, and to prohibit the adjudication of any disputes relating to them? But here we may be stopped by the legal politico-economist with the question—Do you, in this nineteenth century, propose a return to the policy of the fourteenth century? Are you anxious to revive laws which have gone out of date as long ago as the piked shoes and long coats which gave rise to them?

We reply, that we are no advocates for sumptuary laws in general, and that such laws are mostly needless and impolitic; but, in our opinion, legal theories may be safely put aside when they endanger the common rights of humanity. It is one thing to put down piked shoes by a special law, and another to put down murder. The old-fashioned sumptuary laws were directed against foppery, against open and harmless follies, but what we would now advocate is an enactment for the better putting down of secret and villanous crimes.

"*Nec Deus intersit, nisi dignus vindice nodus,*" this is our motto.

We are not ashamed to avow ourselves Gothic enough to wish that the system of extravagant dowers and weddings, stained as they are with innocent blood, should be put down by *authority*. We should prefer that this authority were not extraneous,—that the people themselves, assembled in their *punchayet*, should supply the remedy to their own social evils; but, if need be, we would gladly see the power of the Government employed in supporting the voice of the people.

Let the chiefs of every tribe, whose children have fallen victims to the pride of race, be convened. Their voice will, if we mistake not, be found ready to condemn the time-honoured conventionalities which have led them into crime. If the Government sanction the voice of the people, the Rajpoot will gladly fall back upon such authority, and will fling to the winds the fetters which have so long bound him. One strong and well-sustained effort, and the victory is ours. The voice of nature, the sanction of laws and religion, the common instincts of humanity,—all these are in our favour; and we have but one enemy, *custom*, to overcome. "*Immemorial custom,*" says Menu, the Indian lawgiver, "is *transcendant law,*" and "*the root of all piety;*" and no man who knows India will deny the difficulties of attacking any practice, however absurd or revolting, which has the sanction of custom. But, when custom is quite opposed alike to law and piety, to the law and the religion of the people themselves, it cannot last for ever; the victory, though tardy, will be certain. Here, again, we need not to work in the dark; precedents are close at hand.

We mentioned a few pages back the Choan fort at Mynpoorie. Within a bow-shot of that fort is a prosperous city. The richest and most flourishing families in this city are Brahmins, as rich and prosperous indeed as the Rajpoots are poor and declining. One cause of their prosperity is soon told. Instead of ruining themselves by marriage expenses, they have the strictest sumptuary laws, fixing the amount to be spent at weddings and in dowers, beyond which limit no man can be allowed to spend, or indeed ever thinks of spending, a single rupee.*

We cannot doubt but that the influence of Government might induce the Rajpoots to adopt some similar wholesome rule. Let the Chohan of Mynpoorie and Etaweh, the Kuchwaee of Jyepoor, the Bughela of Rewa and Tirooa, the Rathore of Joudpoor, let all the chief clans of the Rajpoots be convened: let not only the heads of the people, but the heads of ten or fifteen families in each clan, be invited: let them be asked to put down the crime which has so long stained their name. We ask not for mere bonds or promises, but we would have them draw up a moderate scale of dowers, to transgress which shall be punishable. Let such an assembly have the sanction of the Head of the Government, and the days of female infanticide will be num-

* Amongst the Muturrea Brahmins nothing is paid at "lugun," or the period of betrothal. There are four sorts of marriages, called, in the jargon of the tribe,—

| | | |
|---|---|---|
| 1. Awul-bea .. | Soo, Soweya .. | 1st day of marriage ceremonies, Rs. 100. |
| ,, | ,, | 2d payment, Rs. 125. |
| 2. Doem .. | Senkra .. | 1st day, Rs. 50. |
| ,, | ,, | 2d ,, Rs. 150. |
| 3. Teesra .. | Puchisya .. | 1st day, Rs. 25. |
| ,, | ,, | 2d ,, Rs. 50. |

4. Kora .. One rupee is paid by the bride's folk. No disgrace attaches to this cheap wedding.

bered. The penalty itself, and the mode of enforcing it, must be left to the wisdom of the Government to determine. The experiment on a small scale has been tried, and, as it is reported, with entire success. The Mairs (in Mairwara) had long practised female infanticide; but, wishing to give up this custom, they came to Colonel Hall and said, "We intreat you to lower the sum of our wedding contracts; we are unable ourselves to make "the change, but we earnestly beg of you to do so, "binding us all to obedience by heavy penalties." A Convention of the Elders, under the auspices of the Superintendent of Mairwara, was called; and Col. Dixon gives us the result. ("Sketch of Mairwara," p. 31.)

"At this convention it was determined that the Gooroo, or "priest, should receive seven rupees on the celebration of a "marriage; the dholee, or minstrel, forty; and that the remuneration to the bride's father be restricted to 106 rupees. Thus "infanticide received its death-blow through the diminution of "the expense attendant on marriage, which was now brought "within the means of all sections of society. For many "years past no female children have been put to death. The "practice has fallen altogether into desuetude. Indeed, so "greatly have the ideas of the people changed on this and "other usages since the introduction of our rule, that the commission of such an act would now be viewed as a most heinous "crime. Personal advantage has, however, had its weight in "bringing round the desirable reform. Daughters are no "longer looked upon as a source of trouble and anxiety; marriage being open to the poorest classes, they are much in requisition. Hence fathers rejoice on the birth of a daughter, "seeing they are now regarded as a source of wealth."

What has been done by the simple Mairs may

be done, and we believe would gladly be done, by the unsophisticated Rajpoots. Indeed, history tells us that a convention for fixing moderate dowers was held by the Rajpoots under one of their own princes, which failed merely from the want of power of the presiding chief to carry out its decrees. We read in the "Annals of Rajasthan" that the "great chief, Jye Singh of Amber (now Jyepoor), "submitted to the prince of every Rajpoot state "a decree, to be laid before a convocation of their "respective vassals, in which he regulated the "dower and other marriage expenditure with refer-"ence to the property of the vassal, limiting it to "one year's income of the estate. This plan was, "however, frustrated by the vanity of the Choon-"dawut of Saloombra, who expended in the marriage "of his daughter a sum even greater than his sove-"reign could have afforded; and to have his name "blazoned by the bards and genealogists, he sacri-"ficed the beneficent views of one of the wisest of "the Rajpoot race."*

No man has a better right to be heard in any matter affecting the Rajpoot manners than the elegant annalist of Rajasthan; and we have his authority for saying, that a sumptuary edict such as Jye Singh's can alone meet the evils which their marriage customs have entailed. We have just seen

* Colonel Tod helps us here to a precedent from European history, and it is not the only one which might be adduced. "Marseille fut la plus sage des républiques de son temps: les dots ne pourraient passer cents écus en argent, et cinq en habits, dit Strabon."—*De l'Esprit des Loix*, ch. xv.

that in Mairwara Jye Singh's own policy has been revived; that what he could not accomplish has at once been carried out by British influence. Why should not the same experiment be tried on a larger scale? Why need we to despair of the future fates of the Rajpootnee? What India cannot do for her, England can; cast off by her own flesh and blood, where can she better look for protection than to a Government whose power is only equalled by its benevolence? Here she must carry her appeal. The firm hand of British rule, which has rescued the widow from the burning pile, which has shaken off the fetter from the slave, which has given freedom to the humblest peasant under its control, that hand, let us hope, will, ere long, lead the Rajpoot father back to a sense of parental duty. English justice will recover for the Rajpoot's daughter what it has secured for every other subject,—the common blessings of life and liberty.

Since the above Paper was written some further steps have been taken by the local authorities, for an account of which we refer our readers to the subjoined extracts from an Agra newspaper:—

"*Agra Messenger*," *for* 22d *November*, 1851.

We have been favoured with a copy of a set of resolutions passed at a meeting of Chohan Rajpoots in the Mynpoorie district in the present month, and signed by the Rajah and most of the influential chiefs of the tribe. As it will interest many of our readers, we subjoin a free translation of this document.

*Agreement of Chohan Thakoors in the matter of Marriage Expenses.*

"Since many and great evils have arisen in our tribe owing

to the heavy expenses attending the marriage of daughters, we the undersigned write the following agreement, and attest the same (in the presence of the magistrate of our district), of our own free will and accord. According to these resolutions we will act, and will induce others to act as far as we can.

"Resolution 1st.—We will arrange the marriage expenses of our daughters in future according to the following grades:—

"1st Grade.—This is for Rajahs and Talookdars. The maximum to be demanded as dower for a girl shall be rupees 500. One-third to be paid at the period of Lugun, one-third at the door of the bride's father, and the remainder in '*Kuneya Dan*,' Pin money, &c.

"2d Grade.—For Zemindars. Maximum dower to be demanded, Rs. 250; one-third, &c.

"3d Grade.—For persons not Zemindars, in easy circumstances, Rs. 100, &c.

"4th Grade.—For all decent men, one rupee.

"2d Resolution.—If the father of any girl chooses *of his own pleasure* to give more than this, we make no objection—but if the father of any youth *demand* more, we will restrain him; if he insist, we will put him out of our caste as a person who brings dishonour thereon.

"3d.—Brahmins, bards, and barbers, are in the habit of insulting persons who do not spend largely at weddings—we undertake, if such insult be offered to us or our friends, at once to complain to the magistrate, who will, doubtless, prevent abuse being given us.

"4th.—Our wedding procession expenses shall in future be moderate, and according to the grade to which we belong."

The evils alluded to in the preamble are so many and so great, that, as some of our readers know, they have sufficed to overcome the common feelings of humanity, and to cause the destruction of female infants by their own parents. This crime has for some time past attracted the serious attention of the Government and of the local authorities in some districts.

We are inclined to believe that a law for the regulation of dowers, as lately urged upon the Government by a writer in the "Benares Magazine," might be effectual for the repression of the unnatural practices of the Rajpoot clans. But we are not sure whether the plan of *self-legislation*, now, as we learn, adopted by the people themselves, does not at least promise as much as might be expected from any external influences of whatever kind. The idea, too, of destroying one noxious superstition by the instrumentality of another, is worthy of attention. *Caste* has done so much harm in its day, that we shall gladly see its forces turned to the extinction of evils which *caste* itself has produced.

We learn from a witness of the Mynpoorie meeting, that the resolutions which we have detailed were received by the people, not with a mere decent assent, but with hearty and sincere acceptance. This we can easily understand so far as the bulk of the people is concerned, but it can be no easy matter to persuade the chiefs to pass measures which, if thoroughly enforced, must lessen the emoluments and importance of every one of them who has a marriageable son. We think the Rajah of Mynpoorie deserves especial credit for setting the example in so good a work. Nothing, however, can be expected from this movement unless the cognate tribes, the Rahtores, Bhudowreas, Kuchwahas, &c., be induced to unite with the Chohans in the grand work of self-legislation and social reform. We cannot too earnestly impress upon all magistrates the necessity of pushing on a quiet, considerate, yet searching inquiry, into the domestic statistics of the Rajpoots in their several districts, especially as to the numbers of children living, say from ten years and under, of both sexes. It is not in the districts where female infanticide has been most prominently noticed that this crime is most prevalent. On the contrary, it has been checked in those quarters, and perhaps prevails most now where least suspected.

We may return to this interesting, though somewhat difficult subject hereafter. In the meantime, we are glad to hear that the Commissioner of Agra is about to preside at a grand meeting of Rajpoots, to be held at Mynpoorie at the end of this month.

Our views about Government are pretty well known to the public. For European states we should be the last to advocate the delusive advantages of a would-be paternal Government;

but in India we are unable to deny, that a paternal spirit thrown into the administration of public affairs may accomplish much which a mere constitutional policy could never attempt. Nor is it unreasonable to suppose that Englishmen who have proved themselves so well able to walk alone, and choose their own destinies in matters of national policy, may, on the whole, be well trusted to guide and influence the councils of weaker nations. There are cases in which this is particularly clear to the moral sense; and it may be generally affirmed, that whilst constitutionalists will legislate well enough for themselves, when it is their humour so to do, it requires the gentle violence of a paternal rule to lead aright the more wayward and less sophisticated members of the human family. Such, at least, are our impressions after reading the details of the meeting of Rajpoots at Mynpoorie, which is to be found in another part of this day's issue.

These curious tribes are possessed of many good and some great qualities, but their whole character is blighted and marred by the abominable practice, too common amongst them, of "Female Infanticide." The great incentive to this crime is the inordinate expense which attends the marriage of a Rajpootnee damsel. The domestic privacy which these races observe enables them to destroy their newly-born children if they choose, without detection or public censure. Thus, to avoid the expense of marrying a daughter, or the shame of keeping her unmarried at home, the parents make up their minds to put her out of the way, and the unfortunate girls too often find a grave amidst the gloomy galleries of their fathers' strongholds as soon as they see the light.

Much has been done in the way of surveillance to stop this practice; in some districts half of the girls are now saved, and there is reason to believe that continued watchfulness and attention may put down the revolting practices altogether.

In the hope of giving a still more effectual check to crime of this sort, the Commissioner of the Agra division and his subordinate magistrates have, it seems, determined to commence a campaign against those social observances, such as extravagant dowers, immoderate assemblages at nuptial processions, &c. &c.,

which have brought so much injury and dishonour upon the Rajpoot name. If they need encouragement in so sensible a course, they have only to refer to the oft-repeated advice of the present Lieutenant-governor of these provinces, whose object we believe has always been to attack the evil in the bud, and to recommend prevention where cure seems so difficult.

We gave in a late issue of our paper (22d Nov.) an outline of the resolutions to which the Rajpoots of the Mynpoorie district had, at the instigation of the local authorities, subscribed. These resolutions were, it appears, offered by the Commissioner (supported by the judge of the district and the magistrates), to the acceptance of a large body of Rajpoot chiefs, assembled from all the surrounding districts. A large number of these influential men, after fully considering the proposal, put their names to the engagement, which, if as faithfully observed as it was warmly undertaken, will restrict marriage expenses for the future, and thus save the lives of thousands of innocent children.

We are not prepared to say that resolutions so formed and adopted will, of necessity, be binding and effectual; but still, so far as they go, they are good, and, when error is once clearly seen and acknowledged, no one can say that an united protest against such error will be ineffectual. There are some crimes and follies which are checked by the mere notice which publicity may bring upon them.

However, to return to the point whence we started. If we are to have a paternal government for India, let its influences ever be exerted, as on the occasion we are noticing, with the real paternal spirit. When the voice of authority comes forward to plead the same cause as the voice of nature and affection, it will find a ready echo in the human breast.

The Rajpoots of the Doab, who saw the representatives of the Government—men, some of them grown grey in the service of that Government—standing for many long hours whilst they were seated around, until every objection had been met, every question answered, and almost every name affixed to the future charta of their unborn children,—these Rajpoots, we say, will go home to tell their families that, though the Government of their country is in the hand of foreigners, it is carried on, none the less, by men who are neither strangers to their wants nor indifferent to their happiness.

*Mynpoorie.*—On the 5th of this month, this quiet little station was thrown into a state of unusual bustle and excitement. All sorts of Oriental processions, elephants, camels, horses, and ruths, were to be seen converging about noon on the large plain between the Sessions Court-house and the Jail. Hundreds of honest, sturdy-looking pedestrian Rajpoots, each with his tulwar under his arm, were trudging along through the dust which their wealthier chiefs kicked up. All of these men, great and small, had attended the invitation of Mr. Tyler the Commissioner to a grand and solemn meeting, which had been convened by him ostensibly for the purpose of lowering marriage expenses, but in reality with the object of putting down female infanticide, which the said marriage expenses promote.

A long row of tents was pitched for the accommodation of the Rajpoot delegates, open only on one side, facing which was a tent for the accommodation of the Commissioner and other gentlemen attending the meeting. Knowing as I do the pride of the Thakoor chiefs, I watched with some interest this first attempt to get a number of them to consult together on a matter of social policy.

As I expected, when the question was proposed to them where they would please to take their places, each Rajah said that the first place was his due. This matter might easily have been arranged; but there came a worse *nodus*. A man had been invited by mistake, who claimed to sit amongst the Rajahs —one Poke Pal Singh of Awa, in the Muttra district. Poke Pal is not a Chohan, nor a Rahtore, nor a Budhorea, nor a Kuchwaha, but a Jadon. His tribe is considered rather dashed with mongrel blood; and, worse than all, he came to represent not a *real* Rajah, but, as the other chiefs said, a *Company's Rajah*. In short, Poke Pal was a *parvenu*; and the others, who could trace their descent from the sun or the moon, would have nothing to say to him. Matters being thus—the chiefs dispersed in little knots all over the plain, and politely declining the invitation of the Native Deputy-collector to take their places in the *mujlis*—up drove the Commissioner with the Judge,

Magistrate, Joint Magistrate, and other gentlemen who attended the meeting.

The Deputy-collector suggested that the assembly must result in separate groups of the chiefs being brought up to the Commissioner's tent, and matters looked rather unpromising. It was determined, however, to appeal to the politeness of the Thakoors, and very soon all were seated in comfort and good humour round the Assembly tents, or wherever they could find room. Then came the Commissioner, Mr. Tyler; the Judge of Mynpoorie; Mr. Thompson, the Magistrate of Mynpoorie; the Joint Magistrate of Putialee; Mr. Reginald Thornton; Mr. C. R. Lindsay, and other gentlemen who attended the meeting.

In their presence a set of excellent resolutions, which had been previously adopted in the Mynpoorie district, and which have already been noticed in the "Agra Messenger," were proposed to the united assembly. For three or four hours the Commissioner and his party were engaged in explaining and witnessing the signing of these resolutions. The scene was a very gay and rather an impressive one. Most of the chiefs had splendid robes, either of cloth and gold, or brocade; their attendants clustered round with arms, silversticks, chowries. There was the boy Rajah of Mynpoorie on one side just coming into life, a life, too, in his case promising many cares and some dangers; on the other side was another Chohan chief, the old Rajah of Purtabneir, looking already like a mummy, but wrapped up in shawls and brocade. Then came Poke Pal Singh, and close by him, looking very haughty and somewhat disgusted, remarkable by his quaint, conical head-dress, was the manly young Rajah of Rampoor, the chief Rahtore of these parts. Poke Pal Singh spent the morning in informing all passers-by how much the said Rampoor Rajah was honoured and respected by him; the Rajah meanwhile looking uneasy, and paying little heed to the flatteries heaped upon him. Few objections were made, and on all sides terms of approbation were heard. One old gentleman rushed up and said, "It is all very well our signing this, but will the Company let us off our payments at ferries when we go across the water to fetch our brides home?" When the meeting broke up, some three or four hundred names had been affixed to the resolutions, and every chief had thus solemnly pledged his word to assist in the humane object.

Let people, if they like, smile at the credulity of men who believe that the Thakoors are to be trusted; at all events, if one life be spared owing to the exertions of the day, the Mynpoorie meeting will not be unrewarded.

P. S. One Thakoor, a regular old-fashioned Chohan, said to Poke Pal after the assemblage, " No wonder you come here, for now there is a chance for you to get a husband for your daughter." This raised a laugh at the expense of the rich old gentleman, who, it is notorious, had been long offering large sums, ineffectively, to get a Chohan husband for his daughter.

# II.

## THE RISE AND PROGRESS OF OUR REVENUE SYSTEM.

---

THE word Serishtadar, as now used, is probably familiar enough to most of our Indian readers.

It suggests the idea of a comfortable and portly old native gentleman, with a shawl round his waist, a pair of spectacles on his nose, and a bundle of papers under his arm. Sixty years ago, however, it would seem that we had Serishtadars in white jackets and nankin trousers.

Such, at least, does our imagination depict Mr. James Grant, "Serishtadar of Bengal," about the year 1786. This gentleman, in that year, wrote a very valuable revenue paper, called "An Analysis of the Finances of Bengal." We will introduce our subject with an extract from this work :—

"About eleven hundred years since there is some reason to believe that a revolution, introductory of the Brahmin religion and the sway of new rulers, happened, at least in that part of Bengal where the native inhabitants were Budoistes (Buddhists ?) or wholly uncivilized ; as, indeed, may still be said of them, being chiefly of the tribe of chuars, or robbers, of a swarthy black, like the neighbouring mountaineers on the North and West, supposed to be the aborigines of the country."

Supposing Mr. Grant's tradition to be correct, we need not go very far from the famous city whose name our magazine bears,* to seek for the *aborigines* of the country.

A few hours' sail up the winding Ganges will bring us to Mirzapore, the Liverpool of the East. Within sight of its busy market are hills and woods, where these children of the soil find a home and a rough livelihood. There we may still meet them scattered over the country as field labourers, or as freeholders of small patches of land granted by the local chiefs, in acknowledgment of their services as forest-keepers. Some, almost as wild as their neighbour the tiger of the forest, skulk among the rocks and hills forming part of the great Vindhyan chain, and stretching along to the west of the Ganges from Rajmehal to Rotasgurh and Rewah. Others, with habits and superstitions more resembling those of the Hindoo population, inhabit the rough lands which stand between the plains and the hill country. Some have become half Hindoos, others are more than half savages; short in stature, ill-looking, and black, these Coles or Bheels† contrast strongly in appearance with the better-grown and fairer Rajpoot. Miserable though they now be, it is probable that the fair

* Benares.

† Known by various other names, as Koond, Dhangar, Mair, Mina, &c.

plains of India had them as their earliest masters. According to local tradition, a people called Cheroo drove this aboriginal race from the plains to the hills and forests. From the Cheroos sprung that famous tribe called Bhur, Rajbhur, or Bhurputwa, which most undoubtedly occupied the country before the Rajpoots spread themselves over it. Still, to pursue our inquiries in the country about Benares, we find immense mud forts, tanks, and other excavations, which are in that province universally attributed to the agency of the Bhur tribes. If we turn from these mute witnesses of the vigour of a race now nearly lost, to the country people, we shall find that the Rajbhurs hold a permanent place in their myths and traditions. Time-honoured chronicles tell us, for instance, how in the Ghazeepoor district the Rajpoots of Talookah Bahnsdy, were once slaves to the Bhurs; how, when their masters were drunk at a feast, the Rajpoots fell upon them, killing some, enslaving the rest, and dividing the country between the Nirowny Rajpoots of Bahnsdy, the Nihom Rajpoots of Reowtie, the Birwar Rajpoots of Muneer and Mujos, and the Kinwar Rajpoots of Syutwar. So, again, in the Mirzapore district, we learn that Goodun Deo of the Ghurwar family of Rajpoots, from Kanouj, visiting Ramgurh under pretence of pilgrimage, seized upon the country, wresting it from the hands of a drunken and slothful Bhur King. In the Azimgurh* district, too, we shall find traces of the same tribe, the same

* See the printed Report of the Collector of Azimgurh, pp. 7, 8.

immense forts and excavations attributed to the Rajbhurs, or, as they are sometimes called, the Assoors or Demons. The Brahmin* and Rajpoot tribes, by force or fraud, drove away these earlier tribes, a few of whose descendants are still to be found. Sturdy chiefs, like Lot or Abraham of old, divided the land; the jungle disappeared, the swamp was reclaimed by the toil of the military colonists, and the works of cultivation and irrigation began. The sons of the village patriarch, his dependants, the offsets perhaps of some neighbour tribe, united to do him honour and to give him strength. One mess of plain food supplied the males of the ruling family, one stack-yard and granary contained the common treasure of their fields; separate property and separate interests were unknown. To this day, that perfect division and separation of property, which is considered so essential to order and comfort in the Western world, is not fully known amongst these village communities, which, be it observed, in the Bengal provinces have a patriarchal, rather than a corporate character. Even in these degenerate times we could point to bodies of brethren, co-partners, whose horses, cattle, cornstacks,—yes, whose purse even, is common to all. The best feature, however,

* It is probable that the Brahmin families formed settlements in the country before the Rajpoot invasion. For example, we may note that in pergunneh Kantit of the Mirzapore district, where there are 304 estates held by Brahmins, and 308 by the prevailing clan of Rajpoots, the local traditions universally assign the earlier occupation of the country to the Brahmins.

of the Indian village system is to be found not so much in the unity of the brethren, which can hardly be expected to last for ever, as in the policy which admits a severalty of interest, without destroying the unity and continuity of the parent holding. Long heads and honest hearts had those old village worthies who devised a system of rural polity, which, in the northern parts of India at least, has stood alone, unchangeable amidst change, orderly amidst disorder. It is beyond our present purpose to trace in detail the varied and appropriate schemes which the Rajpoot tribes have adopted in their village councils.

Be it enough to observe, that one great object is to maintain every man in possession of the share in the village to which his birth has entitled him; another is to provide for a separation of interests when needful, without a disturbance of the common responsibility of the tribe. We may well believe that men who with their mothers' milk had suckled in the taste of equality and common right, were not to be put off in after life with anything short of their own share, whatever that share may be. If a division of partnership took place by the ordinary laws of the people, all sons shared alike, and the custom of equal inheritance became rooted in their habits.* To this day we find the petty Rajpoot landholder, in connexion with the

* In the families of Hindoo Rajahs this rule does not hold good. With them, generally, the eldest son succeeds to the Raj and to the landed estates.

original unit from whence he and his lands derive their title. He does not claim to own so much land, but so many fractions of that original whole which his ancestor called into separate existence. Thus, so far as we know, grew up and flourished those village commonwealths which give their character to the country. All around tended to attach the military colonist to the soil, to lead him, without renouncing the sword, to cultivate the peaceful arts of husbandry.

The sword, indeed, was not allowed to rust in his hands; martial training prepared the village youth to maintain stoutly what their forefathers had hardly won; a taste for rude freebooting was not entirely kept down by the more chivalrous principles of the clans. At the same time agriculture was the chief avowed occupation of the people, and it was the mixture of agricultural pursuits with a martial and resolute-bearing, which formed the Rajpoot character in that manly mould which it still retains. Their simple plans of life and self-government, their observance of all that habit and custom had sanctified, their determination to assert acknowledged rights rather than to seek to acquire new ones, in short, the genius of their manners and of their religion, tended to bind the village communities closely to the soil. So when the storm of Moslem invasion swept time after time across their fields, the village system rather bent than broke before it. To use the expressive words of one our best and most talented statesmen, the late Lord Metcalfe:—"the village communities are little republics, having nearly everything that they want within themselves, and almost independent of any foreign relations. They seem to last where nothing else lasts. Dynasty after dynasty tumbles down; revolution succeeds to revolution; Hindoo, Patan, Mogul, Mahratta, Sikh, and English, are all masters in turn, but the village communities remain the same. In times of trouble they arm and fortify themselves: a hostile army passes through the country; the village communities collect their cattle within their walls and let the enemy pass unprovoked. If plunder and devastation be directed against themselves, and the force employed be irresistible, they flee to friendly villages at a distance; but when the storm has passed over, they return and resume their occupations. If a country remain for a series of years the scene of continued pillage and massacre, so that the villages cannot be inhabited, the scattered villagers nevertheless return whenever the power of peaceable possession revives. A generation may pass away, but the succeeding generation will return. The sons will take the places of their fathers, the same site for the village, the same positions for the houses; the same lands will be occupied by the descendants of those who were driven out when the village was depopulated; and it is not a trifling matter that will drive them out, for they will often maintain their post through times of disturbance and convulsion, and acquire strength sufficient to resist pillage and oppression with success."

So far we have endeavoured to trace the steps by which the early colonists became owners of the soil. For its peaceable possession they had to pay tribute to the nearest chief who was able and willing to protect them. Such tribute, whether levied in kind from their crops, in coin, or other valuable material, or in gratuitous service and fealty, was, in truth, a sort of black mail levied by the powerful from the weak, as the price of protection. The powerful have in Hindustan, as elsewhere, learned to assert as a right what they could maintain by might. Hence, doubtless, the origin of the king's claim to a share in the produce; a claim readily expanded by obsequious jurists to a share in the soil, or eventually to ownership of the soil. And so in India, as well as in some western nations, we find the theory that the king is lord of the soil. We do not, however, believe that any claim to ownership of the soil was generally pretended by the Hindoo chiefs or kings; they took what they could get, whether a sixth or a fourth, or any other part of the produce; and they collected this their share according to a system of which the traces exist to this day. The Indian genius is fertile in expedients for oppression; one of the oldest seems to be the plan of compromise between the strong and the weak, on condition that the weak should squeeze and coerce those who are weaker still. Whatever be the cause, true it is that the Indian people can only be moved, *secundum artem*, by the lever of one of their own immediate class. Men who would cry aloud for justice, if any other person forced their services, are dragged away from their homes or their ploughs, by the head man or chowdree of their own particular craft, without a word of complaint. Everybody must have noticed the necessity which seems to exist for employing head men, or middle men, in all transactions with the working classes of the East. Be the object great or small, to move an army or to engage a porter, with the aid of the *chowdree* you can get on, without him you are at a stand-still. And so from time immemorial the revenue screw has been applied by the agency of the revenue payers. The local chief called upon the district chowdree for his dues; the chowdree squeezed the head man of the village; the head man in his turn levied the assessment from the village brethren. The regulated-system for collecting the revenue, which thus grew up, though shaken by the violence of the early Mahomedan conquerors, has to this day never been wholly destroyed.

Patans or Moguls were glad enough to avail themselves of a system so economical and so well suited to the genius of the country. When they had leisure* to attend to the collection of the

* The following remarks on the policy of the Moguls, quoted by Rouse in his "Dissertation concerning the Landed Property of Bengal," p. 115, are to the point:—"Les conquérans Mogols porterent dans toutes les contrées qu'ils soumirent par leurs armes un systême de politique qui leur fut prescrit par la néces-

revenue from the land, their desire was to restore the old system; and the reforms which Sher Shah attempted, and the great Akber accomplished, tended to perfect the existing system, not to change it.* Timour ordained, that "if the subjects" (of conquered countries) "were satisfied with the old and established taxes, those taxes should be confirmed."† The Mogul emperors were not slow to acknowledge the expertness of the Hindoos in the varied accounts which were required in the management of the land revenue. Akber owed much of his success, and not a little of his renown, to the labours of his Minister of Finance, the celebrated Tuder Mull.‡ The rules by them prescribed for the conduct of revenue officers are in liberality of spirit, and in justice of intention, not at all behind our most

sité. Au lieu de saisir les terres des vaincus, ils leur en laisserent la possession, pour ne garder entre leurs mains que l'épée: parceque le nombre des conquérans étoit si disproportionné à celui des conquis, que s'ils avoient essayer de se disperser comme cultivateurs dans les diverses provinces, la séparation des membres qui n'eussent plus fait un corps compacte auroit bientôt détruit la puissance de ce peuple. . . . L'ancienne tax constitutionnelle des terres étoit la règle invariable de leurs impôts, en sort que les peuples n'avoient fait que changer des maîtres."—CHEVALIER DE ST. LUBIN. *Politique des Mogols; Mémoires historiques, &c., sur les Révolutions Angloises dans l'Hindustan.*

* See Elphinstone's "History of India," 2d vol. p. 239.

† The amount of these taxes, we learn (see Book II. of the "Institutes" of Timour), was one-third of the produce of irrigated ands.

‡ Tuder Mull was of the Kayeth caste, and early leaving the

modern and approved revenue legislation. Akber desired his revenue collector "to consider himself the immediate friend of the husbandman, to transact his business in a place where every one may find easy access, without requiring any mediator. He must assist the needy husbandman with loans of money, and receive payment at distant and convenient times; he is required to use the utmost circumspection and impartiality in measuring the lands; he is to collect the revenues with kindness, and never make any demands before they become due," &c. &c. * Laws conceived in this liberal spirit, carefully matured and vigorously carried out, left a deep impression on the revenue policy of the country.

A hundred years after Tuder Mull had made his first essay as a revenue officer, we find his system in full force from Delhi to Bengal, under the

Punjab, his native land, commenced his political career in Guzerat, A.D. 1553. He became a military chief and superintendent of revenue by a conjunction of offices common in those days. After serving in Guzerat and in Bengal with reputation, he returned to Delhi in 1577. Here as peshkar, or chief deputy, to the Vizier Shah Munsoor, he assisted in the internal revenue reform with which his name and that of his master, the Emperor Akber, has been associated. Devoid of avarice, and sincere, persevering, even vindictive, in his temper, respected for his attention to the ceremonies of his religion, the character of Tuder Mull gave weight to his measures. He carried out a detailed settlement of the land revenues with equal labour, talent, and integrity.

* "Ayeen Akburee," page 377, Part III. vol. i. Calcutta edition, 4to.

able guidance of Shahjehan.* After Shahjehan came Aurungzebe, from whose time the revenue system began to decline. Let us pause here to notice what a very slight acquaintance with Indian history will teach us, that it requires a great mind to grapple with and master the difficulties of the Indian land revenue system. The greatest generals, the most able politicians amongst the Mahomedans, have been the best revenue officers. When talent and energy were lost amidst a refined and effeminate sensuality, when justice and liberality were forgotten amidst the universal thirst for gold, the revenue administration was the first to suffer. Aurungzebe, though not generally deficient as a politician, made one fatal error: he thrust out the Hindoo officers from all posts of importance in the revenue service. Whilst he was thus wantonly destroying a system which his predecessors had so carefully matured, his rival Sevajee was deeply cementing the foundations of the Mahratta dynasty, by a minute attention to the agricultural prosperity of his conquests. And so, whilst the power of the Mogul declined, the Mahrattas got bolder and stronger, until at last the Emperor of Delhi was a mere captive puppet in their hands.

Let us now glance at a plan of revenue management, which may be termed, for want of a more accurate name, the Zemindarree system. One of

* Shahjehan, however, yielding to the arguments of his able adviser and minister Saadoollah, was inclined to adopt a less detailed mode of collection than Akber had established.

the great principles of Akber's policy was to collect the land tax *directly* from the villagers, without any go-between in the shape of a revenue farmer, and even without a too implicit reliance on the village head man. To carry out the details of this scheme, numbers of subordinate collectors were employed; these were mostly Hindoos, whose patience and skill in accounts qualified them for preparing the various forms required.* With vigorous superintendence, under the eye of a Tuder Mull or a Saadoollah, such machinery would work well. Aurungzebe, however, had not the patience to superintend so vast an apparatus; disgusted with the intrigues of the subordinate Hindoo officers, blinded by an excessive bigotry which could see no need for the services of unbelievers, he dismissed them from their employments. The new men of his own creed lacked the patient diligence and the experience of their predecessors in office. As a matter of course, the order and economy of the revenue collections ceased. A new state of things grew up. It became necessary to issue *sunuds*, or royal patents, for the collection of revenue to contractors, or farmers of revenue, familiarly termed *zemindars*. As the Mogul dynasty drew near to its close, higher and higher swelled the titles—wider and wider rolled the *firmans* of the emperors of the world; but the pompous forms, the fulsome language of the imperial

* See some forty of these forms, many of them containing near fifty columns, in the "Dewan Pusund." Our modern putwarries too are, we believe, expected to prepare numerous forms, giving village statistics in much detail.

edicts, betray the weakness of the body politic, worn out with luxury and enervated by sloth. A crisis was at hand; the healthy vigour which the empire had known in earlier days was lost and gone. It is with empires as with men; the extremities often show the first signs of decay. So we find in Bengal, that, long before the Moguls fell, a complete disorganisation of the revenue system was in progress. The Viceroys, bent on their own selfish and ambitious projects, found it expedient to grasp summarily at the revenue. The regular system was trampled under foot. The provincial governors entered into engagements with men whose talent, wealth, or local influence, best enabled them to extort money from the agricultural population. Thus grew up that class of rapacious powerful contractors for the revenue, the *zemindars* of Bengal, the *talookdars* of the Upper Provinces. The consequences of their arbitrary proceedings were almost fatal to the landed proprietors of Bengal. When the grant of the Dewanny was made to the British in 1765, about a century after the issue of the earliest zemindarree patents, scarcely a vestige of the village communities was in many places to be found. The greater part of the country was found parcelled out into large estates under powerful zemindars. These men, though, as we have seen, in reality merely contractors for the revenue, asserted without scruple proprietary right in their entire domains.

One reason may be given for the common though mischievous error of confounding these zemindarree rights, or rights to collect revenue, with the right of occupation and possession of the lands named in the zemindarree *sunud.* It was natural that the Viceroys, in choosing persons for the office of revenue contractor, should prefer men of local influence and experience. It thus happened that the persons who acquired zemindarree rights were often already endowed with rights allodial and hereditary. The most grasping and unscrupulous of the Rajpoot or Brahmin communities, themselves members of a village community, and at the most only *primi inter pares*, struggled to obtain the imperial patent, with which, when they had got it, they exterminated all rights save their own. Such, at least, was the process in Bengal, which destroyed the village communities. Amongst the sturdier clans of Behar, Benares, and the Doab, the talookdar did his best to imitate the zemindar of Bengal; but his success, owing to the temper of the people, was not so complete. He might harass and depress, but he could not destroy the spirit of the clans. Grants of large tracts in reward of military or political services, occasionally made by the Mahomedans, and frequently by the Mahratta powers, affected the village communities much as the zemindarree grants which we have been describing. Nor were religious and charitable grants over extensive tracts uncommon. In all these cases, it is plain enough that the state can only alienate its own right, viz. the right to collect the land-tax, whether payable in money or in kind. But in the general scramble for wealth and power, which began with the decline of the Mogul emperors, the weakest were trampled under foot, and thousands of landed proprietors became mere tenants at will. In short, when the British began to raise their thoughts from silk pieces and cottons to the magnificent empire which was at their feet, they were fairly puzzled to know to whom the land had belonged, to whom it did belong, to whom it ought to belong. It would be amusing, if it were not sad, to notice the conflicting opinions of those days. Our friend Mr. Grant, the Serishtadar, asserted that all landed property was vested in the State. Mr. Rouse declared that the zemindars were the real owners of the soil. Warren Hastings had one opinion: Philip Francis had another: Shore differed from all. Sorrow came fast upon the communities of Bengal. Worse than sorrow—shame—attaches to the English policy, which at a later period, by dubbing the zemindars as lords of the soil, for ever rivetted the chains which bound down its rightful owners. Hastings would have saved the people and the State from the ruinous measures of the permanent settlement, but he was opposed at home and abroad. When in 1775, ten years after we had undertaken the government of Bengal, he proposed to take some steps towards ascertaining the value and capabilities of the land, he was rebuked by the Court of Directors. In 1781, undismayed by the opposition of his council, and by the ignorant apathy of most of his subordinates, this great man made a last effort to improve the revenue system. Abolishing the provincial councils of revenue, he sent collectors to the several districts in

Bengal. A committee of revenue sat in Calcutta, under the eye of the Government. In 1785, Hastings resigned office; he was succeeded by Mr. Macpherson, whose notions on revenue matters appear to have been sound. It was with the view of restoring the ancient revenue system that Mr. James Grant was appointed to the office of Serishtadar. An enthusiastic admirer of the Mogul dynasty, he would have restored the system of Akber and Tuder Mull. It would, we believe, have been a happy thing for Bengal had his counsels been followed. All sound statesmen in the East saw the necessity for research, before any permanent measures affecting the land revenue could with safety or justice be adopted. Of this necessity no man was better aware than Warren Hastings; but unhappily, at this time, any measure which Hastings approved was at once condemned by a powerful and noisy party in England. Philip Francis had recorded his opinion, that "without a fixed assessment of the land no other measures whatsoever can save the country."* On what data this fixed assessment was to be grounded we cannot tell; but, so far as Francis was concerned, it was not to rest upon the basis of sound experiment and inquiry. With characteristic ignorance of Indian subjects, he opposed every proposal for securing the rights of the Ryots (by which term the ancient village communities were intended) to the perpetual and undis-

* See an elaborate minute of his, stuffed with quotations from Adam Smith, Sir James Stuart, and Montesquieu.—*Revenue Selections*, p. 439.

turbed possession of their lands. In his opinion, it was impossible to support the ryots without doing injustice to the zemindars. Alas that the opinions of Francis should have found acceptance; that those of Warren Hastings should have been rejected! We might wonder that Hastings's common sense was despised, whilst the theories of Francis prevailed, did we not remember that just at this crisis the cry of "India in danger!" was raised. Experience has taught us, that when India is in danger common sense and prudence are at a discount. India in danger! and forthwith some violent remedy is prescribed; generally the catching hold of some new Governor-general, or military chief, who is hurried out to the scene of action with orders to undo all that his predecessor has done. A more high-minded nobleman, a more benevolent statesman than Lord Cornwallis, never existed. But he was sent out burdened with instructions drawn up in London, and ill-adapted to the country in which they were to take effect. A landed gentry, a native aristocracy, a class resembling that which Lord Cornwallis adorned at home, seemed indispensable to the carrying out of the home plans. If such a class was not to be found, it must be created. But the zemindars were surely the very men wanted. Titles, power, wealth, influence they possessed; public spirit, a sense of honour and good faith, would follow when they were liberally and honorably treated. Thus argued Lord Cornwallis, and the zemindars were declared the lawful lords of the soil. This was not enough: their revenue payments to the State must be fixed at once and *for ever!* All measures for ascertaining the value of this apparently inestimable boon were forbidden. Surveys, measurements, and other such ordinary common-sense processes, would not please the young aristocracy;—so thought the Governor-general, and no doubt justly enough. In vain did the mild voice of the experienced Shore plead for delay: in vain did he urge that our limited information forbade a measure so sudden, so vast, and so irrevocable. Cornwallis persisted. The broad lands of Bengal were given away at an unequal and erring rate to the land-jobbing zemindars of Bengal, and for ever! The village communities, who had outlived the convulsions and demise of the Mogul empire, went down to the very dust, to be trampled upon by every village tyrant, to lead a sort of Ishmael life,—their hands against every man, and every man's hand against them. We have called this boon to the zemindars *apparently* inestimable. But there is a fatality attending all attempts at legislating for India in England. Give us English honesty, justice, and independence for India, but spare us English law. By the code which introduced the permanent settlement, it was ruled that before a zemindar could force his tenant to pay his rent, the justice of the demand might be disputed in the civil courts by the tenant, and the payment deferred *pendente lite*. Yet the zemindars were to pay their revenue to Government to the day. The result may easily be imagined; the tenants disputed, the rents were unpaid, the revenue could not be collected, and that monstrous evil, the sale of estates for revenue balances, began. Confusion increased as the lands became the subject of a general scramble. A set of cunning speculators, who had managed to learn enough of the new system for their own ends—rascals, in comparison with whom the zemindars of Cornwallis were respectable, were fast becoming proprietors of the country. The zemindars were falling so fast, that, to save them from annihilation, it became necessary to pass a new law.* This law enabled the zemindar to come down summarily upon defaulting tenants. Some such expedient had been made inevitable by the previous blunders of the legislature. We shudder to contemplate the condition of the tenants, whose forefathers had been in the long enjoyment of landed rights, but who were now given over to a worse than Egyptian bondage. A few extracts from the official records of those days will show whether our language, when mourning over the grave of all agricultural freedom and independence in Bengal, is too strong. The Nizamut Adawlut, the chief court of criminal judicature in the country, informs the Governor-general in 1809,—"We are "convinced that some qualification of the power "now vested in the landholders, farmers, and "under-renters, to recover alleged arrears of rent "by distress, without any previous investigation of "the claim of arrear, is indispensably necessary to "secure the tenants of the land from oppression

* Reg. VII. 1799.

"and ruin."* In 1810, the Magistrate of Dinagepore writes of "a general system of rack-renting, "hard-heartedness, and exaction, through farmers, "under-farmers, kutkunadars (farmers under sub-"farmers), and the whole host of zemindarree "amlah." Even this rack-renting, he tells us, "is "unfairly managed. We have no regular leases "executed between the zemindar and his tenants. "We do not find a mutual consent and unre-"strained negotiation in their bargains. Nothing "like it; but, instead, we hear of nothing but arbi-"trary demands, enforced by stocks, duress of sorts "and battery of their persons."† In 1811, Mr. W. Leycester, Judge of Dinagepore, writes thus:—"The remaining three thousand" (daily prisoners in his district) "I would attribute to the illegal "duress of sundry kinds by the zemindarree amlah "upon the bodies of their ryots, in order to com-"pel some kind of engagement from them which "may be hoped to give a shadow of justice to their "future distraints."‡ The Collector of the district gives similar testimony to the misery of the cultivators.§ In 1815, Mr. Sisson, joint Magistrate of

* Letter from the Register to the Nizamut Adawlut, 4th July, 1809. See, also, extract of a letter from the Acting Judge of Circuit at Moorshedabad, 1st August, 1810. Rev. Sel. 211.

† Magistrate of Dinagepoor to the Acting Judge of Circuit at Moorshedabad, 24th July, 1810. Rev. Sel. 211.

‡ Revenue Selections. 218.

§ Rev. Sel. 231. See, also, a letter from Mr. Barnett, Acting Collector of Rajeshahye, 16th August, 1811. Rev. Sel. 240.

Rungpore, gives to the Government a detailed account of the sufferings of the ryots at the hands of the zemindars, which he concludes in the following words:—"Not a child can be born, not a "head religiously shaved, not a son married, not a "daughter given in marriage, not even one of the "tyrannical fraternity dies, without an immediate "visitation of calamity upon the ryot. Whether "the occasion be joyful, whether it be sad, in its "effects to the cultivator it is alike mournful "and calamitous. Surely it will be sufficient to "have stated these facts. I feel that I should "be only weakening the cause by dispassionately "discussing the probable effects of the continuance of so woeful a system of remorseless "tyranny."*

We admire the independence and honesty with which the civil officers of those days protested against the mischievous policy of Government. Their representations were supported by the Governor-general. The Marquis of Hastings informs the Court of Directors in very plain terms that "The class of village proprietors appeared (in the large zemindarree holdings) to be in a train of annihilation, and, unless a remedy is speedily applied, the class will soon be extinct. Indeed," he adds, "I fear that any remedy that could be proposed would even now come too late to be of any effect in the several estates of Bengal; for the license of twenty years, which has been left to the

* Mr. Sisson's Report, 2d April, 1815. Rev. Sel. 390.

zemindar of that province, will have given them the power, and they have never wanted the inclination, to extinguish the rights of this class, so that no remnants of them will soon be discoverable." It is needless to add to these quotations, but we may well pause to ask, whether the words of Lord Hastings have been prophetic? What are now the rights of the village proprietors in Bengal? Have they been extinguished? Especially we may ask, has the Bengal Government taken advantage of the opportunities given by the survey of the land now in progress to record and to establish such rights as have survived to this day?

The Court of Directors, when it was too late, became aware of the mistakes which had been made in Bengal. For some time after the death of the Marquis of Cornwallis, the system of revenue administration, introduced under his auspices, was considered to be a master-stroke of policy. The sagacious Wellesley applauded it, and hastily promised an extension of the permanent settlement to the ceded and conquered provinces north-west of Bengal.* This promise was renewed by Lord Minto, with the proviso of the sanction of the Court of Directors.† This sanction was never granted. In Lord Minto's time we find the home authorities gradually opening their eyes to the error which they had committed. In 1811, in the strictest terms, they forbade an extension of the

* See Reg. XXV., 1803, and Reg. IX., 1805.

† Reg. X., 1107.

Bengal system to the north-west.* Early in 1812 the Court express a doubt whether, after all, the principle of the permanent settlement be so clearly right as to render its universal adoption desirable. In 1815 their language becomes a little more plain, and "the great mistakes which unquestionably occurred in forming the permanent settlement" are commented upon freely enough. In short, the bubble had burst; the permanent settlement was found to have been a mistake.

Thus far we have endeavoured to trace the origin of landed property, such as we now find it, in the Bengal presidency, and we have noted the effects of the permanent settlement upon the landed proprietors in Bengal proper. Turn we now to the north-west. Gradually, as we recede from Bengal, setting our faces towards the sources of the Ganges, we begin to meet with men of stouter frame and tougher texture. And now, as at length we stretch over the vast level Doab between the Ganges and Jumna, we find ourselves amongst those soldier-cultivators, whom we have described in the graphic terms of Lord Metcalfe.† Bred under a severer climate, agriculturists and soldiers by taste, sometimes robbers from necessity, the clans of the north-west, through every political storm, have clung fast

* "The object of the present dispatch," says the Court, "is "to caution you in the most pointed manner against pledging "us to the extension of the Bengal fixed assessment to our newly "acquired territories."—*Letter to the Bengal Government, 11th November*, 1811.

† Ante, p. 46.

to their village lands. Time will not permit us to dwell at any length on the details of our earlier administration in the ceded or conquered provinces. An extension of the permanent settlement, as we have already observed, had been promised *unconditionally* by Lord Wellesley, and *conditionally* by Lord Minto. The condition was the sanction of the Court of Directors, who, very fortunately, did not grant it. Lord Minto hinted at "*the dangerous consequences* to be expected from the disappointment of the landholders of the upper provinces if the boon were longer delayed." But the Court had grown wary, and as for the landholders, the sample they got of the Bengal revenue legislation in the operation of the land sale laws which had been introduced was quite enough for them; in fact, when some years later the Marquis of Hastings made a tour through the provinces—a tour, too, for the very purpose of inquiry into the condition of the landed classes—we believe that he was not once reminded of the promises of Lord Minto or Lord Wellesley. The Marquis by this time was aware, that there would be more of danger in attempting to introduce the Bengal policy than in declining to extend it to the north-west. Up to the year 1822, if the acts of the (Revenue) legislature had been feeble and uncertain, so had the proceedings of the executive been most faulty, perplexed, and irregular. Do we blame the early servants of Government if their acts were arbitrary, their councils irresolute? Certainly not; our early commissioners and collectors in the north-west were working in the dark, or, at best, were as mariners in a troubled and dangerous sea without chart or compass. Ignorant of the tenures of the country, they were obliged to trust to powerful and interested subordinates, who led them astray. Or when, in spite of obstacles, they had gained something of local knowledge and experience, their hands were tied by the laws which they administered.

That *monstrum horrendum*, the sale-law of Bengal, had been imported; a law alike unsuited to the habits, feelings, and genius of the people, and, as we believe, to the real interests of the State. The scramble which had taken place in Bengal was acted over again in the north-west. But the stout Rajpoot was not to be tamed like the effeminate Bengalee. A war of land-holder against decree-holder, auction-purchaser, and all other intruders, began, which has left indelible marks upon the history and condition of the people at large. Law failing, luck failing, the stubborn husbandman had recourse to the last argument,—indeed, too often the first argument with a Rajpoot,—the club or the tulwar. Open affrays, nightly assassinations, endless and bloody feuds, spread over the land. All the clubs and swords, however, could not deter sharp men from studying our revenue practice, in order to obtain a title to lands. The excitement of the ordinary law courts was tame compared with that which our revenue officers afforded. As the sale-day came round, whilst the defaulting landholder was either kept by the contrivances of the officials in ignorance of his liabilities, or was sulkily abiding the doom of his lands in his old ancestral fort, the sleek money-dealer was at his post; the lot was proclaimed, bribes went round, knowing looks passed between the amlah and the capitalist, whilst the collector's hammer transferred estates, equal, perhaps, in extent and value to a first-rate German principality, from a family of fine fellows, whose forefathers had reclaimed it from the wild beasts, to some cunning usurer, who would never have the heart to visit his purchase. At last, one of the magistrates,* a benevolent and talented man, protested in language so powerful, yet so just, against these proceedings, that the Government were obliged to interfere. A regulation was passed, with the express object of cancelling the iniquitous proceedings by which "poor and ignorant men" had been, under cover of the sale-law, deprived of their property.† Let us hope that the special commissioners appointed under this law did some good and remedied some evil. Better times were now fast approaching. One most important discovery had been made. We had learned our own ignorance. At last the Government fully felt the necessity for inquiry and investigation. The result of Holt Mackenzie's tour with the Governor-general, through the upper provinces, was the enactment of Regulation VII.

* Mr. T. C. Robertson, afterwards Lieutenant-governor of the Agra Presidency.

† Reg. I., 1821.

of 1822. This was the Magna Charta of the village communities. From its date commences a new era in the revenue history of India. Property in the soil, as distinguished from interest in the *mal* or revenue, was, for the first time, clearly recognised. The collectors were set to work, and plenty of work was cut out for them. The interests of all parties connected with the soil were to come under revision and record. The various claims to the land, some concurrent and requiring specification, some conflicting and demanding settlement, were to be reviewed. Inquiry was to be pushed close as to the productiveness and capabilities of the soil. Holt Mackenzie's anxiety to do justice to all, to a certain extent, defeated its own object. An amount of detail and of labour was thrown upon the collectors which was more than they could bear. Fast men could make little progress in the settlement of their districts; slow men made none at all that was perceptible. Nor could it be otherwise with proceedings so varied and so minute. A hide of land supplied a bullock-load of records. Before many years had passed, the revenue machinery, which had seemed to Mackenzie rusted with idleness, was found clogged with over-work. Thus stood matters when Lord William Bentinck's powerful and practical mind was brought to grapple with this great question. He determined, if possible, to remedy the stoppage, and, calling to his aid one of the ablest men in the Civil Service, he applied himself to the work.* A short, but stringent and effectual, law was passed.† The impossibility of bringing disputes to a crisis had hitherto stopped surveys, settlements, and everything else. A remedy, simple and equitable, was provided. The collector was empowered, in disputed cases, to summon a village jury, and to carry out their award at once. Another cause of delay had been the enormous demand upon the collector's time and patience for the arrangement of minor details. These were wisely handed over to native or other qualified subordinates, with powers to act as deputy-collectors. No effort, no expense, was spared to set on foot that great and noble work, *the survey and settlement of the north-western provinces.* Under the auspices of Lord Bentinck the chief Board of Revenue gradually matured their plans. With the aid of some of the best talent which the Service could supply a scheme was completed, which to the scope and liberality of Akber's policy added the exactness of European science. The work was carried out ably and zealously, and eight years saw every village in the north-western provinces measured, every field mapped. We must satisfy ourselves by hastily no-

* Our great revenue reformers have not always been trained in any existing revenue school. Monro laid down the sword to introduce the ryotwar system at Madras. Holt Mackenzie belonged to the Secretariat; and Robert Martens Bird, before he was called to the Revenue Board by Lord William Bentinck, had on the judicial bench become acquainted with the defects of our revenue system.

† Reg. IX., 1833.

ticing the points of difference which are most obvious, when comparing this settlement with that of Bengal. And though the contrast, if fairly drawn, must show in strong colours the superiority of the later operations, it must be remembered that nearly fifty years had elapsed since the earlier settlement was devised. If, with more mature experience, we were able to avoid the rocks upon which our earlier legislators ran, it is but fair to acknowledge that the same just, liberal, and honest intention pervaded the early and the late settlement. The difference was in the head, not in the heart, of the great men whose policy we are discussing. The philosophy of the first settlement was that of the old schoolmen; a dogma was taken up, and matters were driven into agreement with it. The philosophy of the last settlement was of the inductive method. Holt Mackenzie and Robert Bird are the Bacons and Hookers of our revenue schools. The projectors of the first settlement forbade and eschewed local inquiries of a close and searching nature. They forgot the ground on which they stood to look for analogies which had no existence. Full of theoretical justice, they did solid wrong; full of real benevolence, they spread ruin and desolation around. The projectors of the last settlement, by a wide observance of the real state of things, by comparison, by analysis, by patient investigations, qualified themselves to take up solid ground, and on it to build a stable and well-proportioned structure. The first settlement ruined the persons for whose benefit it was devised. The last settlement saved millions of much-enduring men from ruin and misery. The ancient landed proprietors were protected from further injury and degradation. In numberless cases they were restored to their rights —rights which, though they had never ceased to assert, they had almost despaired of asserting with success. In Bengal, the mass of the agricultural communities were given over, tied hand and foot, to *soi-disant* zemindars, who had no real and paramount rights, and no bowels for the people. In the north-west, the agricultural classes were released from the thraldom in which they had been held by revenue farmers and contractors, whether known as Rajahs or Talookdars. Considering the process by which these talookdars had obtained a footing over their estates, it would have been perfectly justifiable if the ruling power had declined their further services as middle-men, and forthwith removed them from all holdings to which they could not prove a title by inheritance or purchase. Nay, not only would such a process have been justifiable, but some such restitution justice demanded in favour of the families who, during the last half century, had sunk under the power of the talookdars, almost to the level of mere tenants at will. Justice was done, but justice was tempered with mercy. A selfish policy would have supported the talookdars and quietly extinguished the subordinate proprietors, if, indeed, they can be justly called subordinate who were, though oppressed, the real lords of the soil. Stern justice might have ousted the talookdars and have restored the village communities, as we have already said, leaving the talookdar to fall back upon such resources as he might have, independently of his talookdaree rights. But the Government did not press so hardly upon men, who, though without sufficient title, had long enjoyed power and wealth. In the large talookas the villages were settled with such of the local communities as could prove a just title to the land; the State took all the risk and all the loss attendant upon engagements with broken, thriftless, and impoverished men: but, at the same time, a considerable allowance (from 10 to 30 per cent on the revenue payments) was settled on the excluded talookdar. For this act of self-denying justice, which brought liberty and comparative independence to thousands, we conceive that the revenue authorities deserve all credit. A more just, and, as one would suppose, a more popular measure, could not have been devised. Yet, both in India and in England, this particular part of the settlement proceedings has been suspected and abused. At home, the matter was never fairly understood, except by a very few of those who had to pass an opinion upon it. In India we might well wonder that the enfranchisement of the village communities was unpopular, unless we happened to know what Indian popularity means. The *vox populi*, we may at once say, has little or nothing to do with it, for that voice is not yet heard. In a country where public spirit and patriotism are unknown, and where tyranny has long pushed law aside, a Government, to be good, must be paternal. A just and powerful Government, whose aim is

> "Parcere subjectis et debellare superbos,"

will only be popular when the popular voice has had time to gain confidence, and to create an audience for itself. Spurious popularity in the East may be cheaply obtained by following Sir Robert Walpole's maxim, "*quieta non movere*." Let the rich devour the poor, let the powerful oppress the weak, touch not vested interests, and with a little courtesy and professed liberality, a Government will be popular.

The voices of those who alone obtain a hearing, because they alone can make themselves heard—the voices of the great, the rich, and the influential, will join in a chorus of adulation. But let the sword which God has placed in the hand of the magistrate be fearlessly wielded, let impartial justice be shown to all alike, and there will be an end of popularity. Millions may bless, and will bless, an intrepid and just Governor; but then who, in India, hears the voice of the million? No, it must be an object more real and noble than popularity which nerves the legislator for his task. It must be a sense, a deep and earnest sense of duty. This eminently did those men possess who planned and executed the settlements in the north-west. Their chief objects were to equalise the burdens borne by the landed classes, to rescue and record the rights of the village communities, and to introduce fairness and moderation in the transactions between landlord and tenant.

It is impossible to deny that their efforts have been successful. There is at present a lucid order and economy about the revenue system to which no other branch of the administration can pretend with any sort of justice. Our Police, our Civil Courts, might well be improved; our revenue management in the north-west seems alone to progress steadily towards excellence. A reform so great and so rapid must in its course meet with opposition, and give cause for hostility. Amongst the servants of Government, some of the most estimable, whose station and habits removed them from much contact with the mind of the people, took their estimate of the settlement from their native acquaintance amongst the higher ranks.

There may have been other reasons, too, for the prejudice with which some of what may be called the old school regarded this great measure. With them we seek no controversy. Nor will we stay to dispute the point with those who call the necessary lowering of the Government demand, owing to the effects of the lamentable drought and dearth of the years 1837 and 1838, a breaking down of the settlement. We care not to argue with opponents who attribute the visitations of God to the devices of man. Let such take their stand with the gentleman at Bombay, who has traced the ravages of the cholera to the salt monopoly of the East India Company. But, in truth, now that the improved revenue system has had time to work, and to prove its worth, it needs no apology or defence. The greatest happiness of the greatest number has, as far as possible, been secured. The exact state of things in every township has been carefully investigated and recorded. Disputes have been composed; jealousies have been allayed. The rights of the village sharers have been carefully preserved and recorded, whilst the interests of the merest cultivator have not been overlooked. The orderly payment of a moderate revenue has been provided for, and where default occurs, the means have been devised for coming down directly upon the defaulter, and saving the man who has discharged his engagements punctually. In every district, officers selected from the people decide every dispute that may arise, under the direct control of the Collector of the district. Check upon check has been devised to prevent delay in the decision of all cases affecting the interests of the landed community. And as, in an operation so vast as the settlement of these provinces, many errors and inaccuracies must have crept in, the revenue authorities have been invested with power to rectify any error and to supply any deficiency in the record.* Of late years, the best energies of the Government have been directed to the improvement and consolidation of the revenue system. Compendious treatises, embracing not only the rules of revenue process, but also the principles of revenue science, have been drawn up. Translations of these have been distributed right and left.

The more intelligent of the people are being thus fast led to co-operate with their rulers, whose

* See Government resolution, 12th September, 1848.

principles are better understood and appreciated. All candidates for government employ find the necessity of mastering the existing Revenue Code.

The consequence is, that numbers of books in the language of the country, some of considerable merit, are issuing from the presses at Agra, Delhi, and elsewhere, explanatory of the laws affecting landed tenures, and of the principles of agriculture and rural economy.

The Collectors of Revenue have been encouraged to disseminate manuals of useful knowledge suited to the capacities of the rising generation among the students at the village-schools. Such books, for which also the people have to thank the Government of the north-western provinces, will, we trust, supersede the trash which has hitherto been taught at these schools.

One great work remains to be noticed, the importance of which to the physical welfare of the millions of the Doab can hardly be over-rated. In these fertile, but thirsty plains, the demand for water is almost incessant and unlimited; in seasons of drought the whole country becomes panic-stricken. Thousands snatch their means of subsistence direct from the soil, who, when their crops fail for want of rain, have nothing to subsist upon. Grain may be stored in abundance, but the smaller landholders have nothing to give in exchange for it. Famine and pestilence are the necessary consequences; nor can all the liberality of Government do much to avert the evil.

It has been reserved for an administration identified in a peculiar manner with the revenue reforms in the upper provinces to commence upon this great work, and to urge its progress, in spite of many obstacles. The Ganges Canal will, when completed, save the Doab from future dread of famine—as a magnificent proof of British enterprise it will, we trust, ere long take its place with the survey and settlement operations. Pointing to these monuments of the energy, the skill, and the liberality of the British Government in India, we shall be able confidently to boast that the mantle of Akber has fallen on no unworthy successors. In Akber's imperial city shall the fame of Akber be eclipsed. It may, haply, belong to Agra to roll away the reproach which has been too long attached to the British name, the reproach of narrow commercial views and selfish policy. As the friends of India, above all, of the patient cultivators of the soil, the best wish we can offer them is that Englishmen may fulfil their high destinies. Conquerors of all around, a noble strife is yet before us. A glorious battle is to be fought, not in tented field, not in the arena of ambition or self-aggrandisement. England's remaining combat must be, not only with the cunning, the ignorance, the superstition of her Eastern children, but with the pride, the sloth, the selfishness of her own sons. In such a warfare, conquering ourselves, we shall conquer all. Justice, mercy, and Christian charity,—these must be the weapons which, steeling our own hearts, and softening the hearts of our opponents, shall surely bring us to victory.

## III.

### CHARACTER OF THE RAJPOOT AGRICULTURIST, AND CONDITION OF THE LANDED PROPRIETORS UNDER BRITISH RULE.

---

An intelligent traveller from London or New York, arriving in Calcutta, and taking up the papers of the day in the hope of gleaning some information about the country and people, would probably find himself fairly puzzled. In one column he would read a sprightly article, in which the settled superiority of British rule over Indian anarchy was touched with the passing pen, as a matter of fact, open to no dispute, and requiring no confirmation. In the next page, however, if he did not meet with the direct converse of this proposition, he would probably be told plainly enough that the sway of the English in India was a mere pretence or a palpable failure. The more he read, the more his wonder would grow. How comes it, he might ask, that an empire confessedly so magnificent, the envy and wonder of the world, a whole evidently so stupendous, is yet made up of parts, which, if the public prints are to be believed, are ill assorted, worse put together, and separately contemptible? If the Government be feeble and partial, the courts venal, the police corrupt; if all the machinery of the State be out of order, and all its functions deranged; how comes this general confession, whether avowed or implied, of the depth, the supremacy, of British influence in the East? We might attempt to solve this question by asking another. Is the English public able to judge fully and impartially of the condition of the Indian people? India owes much to a free, and, on the whole, an enlightened press, which by boldly recording facts has drawn attention to long-established grievances or to incipient abuses; but in the nature of things the British press is better able to protect and define the rights of Englishmen than to decide that great and momentous question, *the condition of the people of India*. Yet the test by which Government must be tried is this: Are our laws and institutions suited to the genius, happiness, and improvement of our subject millions? Before this question, which we must answer one day to God and to man, other matters sink into comparative insignificance. We believe that the efforts of the Government to suit their proceedings to the people have of late years been great; but, owing to the nature of our empire in the East, these efforts are but little known and much misrepresented. The powers that be are the constant objects of attack here, as indeed in all free countries, or in all countries in which the press is unshackled. But in Europe and America, where party spirit reigns supreme, if one party attacks the Government another defends it; and the State gains as much by his friends as it loses by its foes. Here it is all attack and no defence. Our Indian Governors, conscious of material power and full integrity of purpose, guide calmly and steadily the vessel of the State, and scorn to shorten sail to the puffs of calumny, with a degree of stoicism which we believe may be carried too far: they resent no injury, repel no insinuation, and invite no aid.

We have been led into these reflections by the examination of a little treatise on village affairs, which has lately been published at Agra.* This work adds one to the many proofs around us of the valuable results of our improved revenue legislation. A native of talent and observation, who, under the old régime could never have risen to any share in the revenue administration, now speaks *ex cathedrâ* as a deputy-collector, and in a lucid sketch of the internal village state gives us the result of his experience. We turn to this subject with interest, because we believe that our late success in the revenue administration is little known to the English public, and has not been yet sufficiently appreciated. The subject is not only interesting in itself, and by no means exhausted; but is also so pregnant with suggestion as to what our general policy should be, that its indirect importance can hardly be over-

* *Kitáb i hálát i Dihee*, or the Book of Village Affairs. By Jumaloodeen Hussun, deputy-collector of Mynpoorie. 1850. Lithographed (in very good style) at the Musdir-ool Nuwadir Press.

rated. The nature of our present revenue system, and the reason of its success, may be shortly told. Our plan is, after patient inquiry into the condition of the people, into their own way of thinking and acting, to form rules of procedure which may suit existing and deeply-rooted institutions. Instead of trying to force these institutions into a model which may suit our ideas of expediency, we have of late years tried earnestly to adapt our proceedings to the wants and the genius of the people. This is the secret of our success, and the omen of our future increasing strength and prosperity. Working with the people of the country for their good, Heaven will bless our labours, and we may accomplish the great destiny which opens before us.

Our present object is to give some slight idea of the existing state of the agricultural proprietors under our rule in the north-western provinces. The leaders amongst them are the descendants of those colonists, half-soldiers, half-cultivators, whose origin we attempted to trace in a former number.* These form, perhaps, the most important, and certainly not the least interesting, portion of that vast family which has fallen so strangely under the sway of the Anglo-Saxon race. Men like these are worth examining ; their almost mysterious origin and settlement, their manly mould and character, their soldierly bearing and ancient blood, alike commend them to our sympathy and our respect. Such, in many points of resemblance, were the fathers of our

* See No. II. p. 41.

own island home. Here, in the far East, we may trace the clannish feelings and feuds, the love of a ride across the border, the readiness for an appeal to sword or club, which marked our Celtic progenitors. Here, again, we may note the endurance of toil, the tenacity of purpose and affection, the devotion to the household gods, the homestead, and the soil, which our Saxon fathers knew. It may be as well to select, as a fair specimen of these tribes, the Rajpoot of the Doab.

The traveller passing up towards the north-west, from the sacred spot where, under the walls of Allahabad, the Ganges and Jumna unite, must not expect to see anything like a beautiful country. For, in truth, whatever there may be of sylvan or rural beauty in the Doab, does not disclose itself to the wayfarer on the high road. The highway itself, with its stream of varied life, may interest; the general look of the country will only give disappointment. Yet, if you strike off the beaten path at any point from Allahabad to Delhi, you can scarcely go many miles without coming upon scenes of much quiet beauty. Villages, surrounded at one season with the richest vegetation, at another with golden crops, throw an air of rural comfort and abundance over the scene. The mango grove, the tank, the village shrine, adorn a landscape, which, if not beautiful, is at least pleasing to the eye. The most prominent object in such scenes is the old village fort, which has for centuries sheltered some clan of Rajpoots, half-kings, half-robbers. Passing the underwood in which cattle are grazing, the lotus-covered pond, the groves and orchards which cluster around, you come to the stronghold whose rising towers look over the surrounding plain. The approach is by a rough steep track, worn deep with the feet of men and cattle. The thick bamboo jungle which once surrounded the walls has been cut down, the moat has been nearly filled up with the rubbish of a century, the massive doors have fallen into decay; but still there is a rough kind of stateliness, a sort of baronial dignity, hanging about the place. Pushing through a wicket you come, under a heavy gateway, into the quadrangular inclosure within the walls. Here all tells of rural abundance, and of the *dolce far niente* of country life. On one side are buffaloes and cows tethered, lazily chewing the cud, or eating their provender out of huge earthenware vessels let into the earth; on another side is a range of stabling for horses, bullocks, or other cattle. Here a long open passage is filled with the palanquins and bullock-carriages of the family; there stands a row of closed chambers, stored with the produce of the farm, heaps of grain, oil-cake, or sugar in great reservoirs of unbaked clay, defying damp and vermin. At the further corner of this inclosure is a rough stair, leading up to the flat roofs of the stables and storehouses below. Here are the lounging-places, the beds of the male members of the family, and chambered galleries, leading away to the more private abodes of the women. Your Rajpoot is not very choice about his bed-room or bed, and is satisfied with any corner in which the wind blows upon him, where he can find a place to hang up his trusty sword and buckler close at hand. For a seat he has a great clumsy wooden platform, or a cart-wheel set up upon legs. The most luxurious have nothing better than a carpet or rug, with great pillows of red cloth, stuffed with tow or cotton, of which the shape and size would make an English upholsterer stare. Furniture, besides what we have described, there is none; but in the recesses of the wall you may see, perchance, a bundle of dusty papers, a powder-horn, an inkstand, and perhaps the picture of some god or hero. Pigeons fly in and out of little boxes fastened against the walls, and perhaps a stray, melancholy-looking peacock, stalks, sentinel-like, along the galleries. The sacred peepul or banyan-tree has been taught to climb across the roof, throwing a pleasant shade around. In a quiet corner, as you stoop to look into the deep cool well, the sudden dropping of a curtain, and the clank of a bangle, tell that the female apartments are not far off.

It is, perhaps, a natural error which the Rajpoots make when they mistake exclusiveness for civilisation. Proud, ignorant, and select, they are exclusives *par excellence*. The sword cannot cut its way into their set, neither talent nor even money can force its barriers. Railway scrip may bring a small tradesman in England to hob and nob with a Duke, until it be convenient to kick the *parvenu* down stairs again; but our Indian gentry are not so accessible. However, exclusive though they were, the Rajpoots of the olden time did not deny the light of heaven to their wives and daughters; it was the jealous Mahometan who taught the Hindoo to be as suspicious of his women as he already was scrupulous of his caste. So now it is the lot of the females to be kept in doors, and to be huddled up in some corner if a stranger of the other sex come near; and instead of going about openly and fearlessly, as was once her custom, the Rajpootnee is early taught to affect the airs of the Zenaneh. Having, however, a naturally strong turn for domestic and rural economy, the women, though ignorant, are not idle or useless. They grind the corn, make the bread, look after the dairy produce, and, except amongst the proudest clans, spin cotton-thread for household use; these pursuits, with the care of their children, and other inferior domestic duties, keep them employed. With these occupations, and perhaps from the necessity of the case, the Rajpootnee generally keeps faithful to her lord; if she admit a stranger to her favours, it is at the risk of her life. Every Indian magistrate knows that the Rajpoot, at no time very placable, *never* forgives and seldom cares to survive conjugal dishonour. Instances are frequently occurring of men who, on suspicion of intrigue, fall upon the offending woman, murder her, and then sullenly give themselves up to justice, with the remark that their honour is gone, and the sooner their life goes the better. His sense of honour, keen, perhaps morbid, would lead a Rajpoot to defy a thousand deaths rather than to proclaim his shame in courts of law. A sweep of his sword frees him from the *vinculum matrimonii*, or from any rival who may venture to trespass on forbidden ground;

that done, he is ready to die himself, and, as we have already said, seldom cares to live under his disgrace. So long as his wife behaves well, he is a faithful and often an indulgent husband. As a parent, we must look at him from two separate points of view, if we can. He is very fond and proud of his sons. His daughters—alas! it is no secret how they are treated. We remember a sermon on "Cruelty to Animals" by the celebrated Chalmers, in which he proved that this crime was to be attributed rather to the negative qualities of inattention and want of sympathy, than to any active spirit of hate, or of blood-thirstiness, in the human breast. We are not going to apologise for the Rajpoots, who allow their daughters to be destroyed like blind puppies; but we believe that their crime is quite as much the result of want of principle as want of affection. The proof of this is, that if once their daughters are spared, the fathers become as fond of them as they are of their boys. However, be this as it may, it is impossible to deny the existence of the fearful crime of female infanticide amongst many of the Rajpoot tribes.* Such a practice can only be stopped by reforming the

* The reasons why the higher castes of Rajpoots murder their girls are various. The chief inducement to this crime is the heavy expense to which their customs expose them on the occasion of the marriage of a daughter. These may be thus stated. On the conclusion of a match between the parents, a sum of money is sent to the father of the youth by the father of the girl. This sum is not large, probably about the tenth of the amount of "Juheez" or dower. This is a sort of earnest-

people, or by coercing them: coercion would only avail when founded on a system of rigid espionage, most intensely odious to the feelings of the people. The British Government have preferred the attempt to reform, to the determination to put down this secret wickedness; and to a certain extent they have succeeded. Forgetting, if we can, this dark stain in the character of the Rajpoot father, it is only just to add, that when the natural feelings are allowed to have play, there is no want of deep and

money; and when the ceremony of "Tilluk" is completed, the father of the girl cannot recede from the engagement.

After this comes the "Luggun," when half of the dower agreed upon is paid, and the date for the nuptial procession, called the "Burat," is settled. The "Burat," or chief marriage ceremony, to which all the relations and friends are invited, is the occasion of the most profuse expenditure in feasting them; the greater the multitude fed, the better satisfied is the pride and vanity of the father of the girl, who at the same time pays the remainder of the dower. This sum varies according to the rank of the parties, but is generally enough to throw the father into debt and difficulties. Unless a handsome sum be offered, a husband of good caste is not to be procured; and unless the feasting be profuse and the invitations to the marriage-feast general, then the girl's parents are held up to public scorn, as stingy or poverty-stricken. This is the chief reason why the high-caste and proud Thakoors hate the idea of a daughter being born to them. Another reason is the blind pride which makes them hate that any man should call them Sala or Sussoor, Brother-in-law or Father-in-law.

This crime of infanticide is not confined to the Rajpoots. Some tribes of the Aheers are equally guilty. We remember remonstrating with the heads of an Aheer village, who had ten girls to eighty boys living. They said, "Sir, it is all very well for Bunyans and such people to beget girls, but they are very seldom born to men of our caste."

disinterested paternal and filial affection. Education, so far as letters are concerned, they have not themselves, and they seek it not for their children, beyond what may enable them to scrawl their names in unequal characters, or to puzzle out a few Hindee rhymes. Moral education, properly so called, is not to be expected amongst men whose religion is independent of any real moral law. To supply in some poor degree these defects, we find amongst them a reverent observance of the various forms and obligations, whether domestic or social, which time and custom have sanctified. From these laws, such as they are, there is no appeal; and opinion, call it public or private, exercises a most tyrannical sway over the Hindoo mind. It is hardly the fault of the Rajpoot of the present day, however much it may be his misfortune, that the public voice, to which he alone can be expected to listen, calls light darkness, and darkness light. Whilst we deplore his ignorance we must yet admire his virtues, virtues marred yet not utterly destroyed by an evil superstition. As a whole, his character is a fair type of what fallen man unaided by Divine teaching must ever be; a ruin, but still with a touch of native majesty clinging about it. Laborious without method, frugal without economy, and chaste without principle, he is by turns generous and malignant, affectionate and cruel.

There is no progress about this race. Calcutta Baboos may ape English vices, may read the "Age of Reason," and sup off ham and champagne;

country dealers and artizans, petty lawyers and publicans, may push on and gather wealth, to spend it in luxury; the Rajpoot looks on unmoved. Money he may desire, but not for the material luxuries which it can command. He has few wants, fewer aspirations: a mess of unleavened bread and vegetables, a few curds and sweetmeats, are enough for his food; a dress of quilted cotton for winter, of white cloth for summer, with a turban for holidays, these supply his wardrobe. He seldom seeks for any stimulants more powerful than tobacco, or any greater luxury than his hookah. On the whole, though his conduct is regulated by no real moral principle, it is correct and decent, and you cannot help liking the man, though you cannot quite respect him. He is a fast friend and a bitter enemy, a strange mixture of nature and sophistication. Land he dearly loves, because of the power which landed possessions confer, and the pride which in all countries they feed; and, except his honour and his son, there is nothing perhaps so dear to him as his land.

When the Rajpoot stalks forth from his home to the village council, where, under the shade, the elders of his race are assembled, he is easy and good-natured in his temper so long as he observes no attempt upon his rights. If, however, he suspect unfair treatment, he soon gets noisy and excited; opposition makes him violent; treachery, revengeful. In old times, right gave way to might, and clubs and swords were quickly brought to bear upon a disputed point. Now, after an inordinate amount of clamour, the disputants gird up their loins and set off to the collector's cutcherry. Before we attempt to follow them there, it will be well to trace some of the more prominent features of the village constitution; in doing which, we shall avail ourselves gratefully of the useful forms of village accounts which Jumaloodeen Hussun's book supplies. Perhaps the history of a village in the Doab for the last fifty years may serve to place our object in a clear light.

Runjeet Singh was a Rajpoot of the last century. He and his elder brother left home young, after an unsuccessful struggle for their rightful share of the land, and in the early part of the present century were amongst the most conspicuous of Lord Lake's native cavalry officers. After the battle of Laswarree, in which his elder brother fell, Runjeet retired from the army with a shot through his leg, a pension, and what we call in England a comfortable independence. The old soldier determined to change his rupees into land. In the early days of British occupation he had not much difficulty in suiting himself with a couple of snug estates. In one of these, called Rajpoor, he took up his abode with his two sons, Shere Singh and Baz Singh. It was a pleasant spot this Rajpoor, with its fine old trees hanging over the banks of the Ganges. The other village, called Futtehpoor, lay in that rich well-watered valley, along which the Kallee Nuddee runs, between Furuckabad and Mynpoorie. It is with Futtehpoor we have most to do. The lands had been tilled for ages, partly by a number of cultivators of the Kachi caste, and partly by bearers and fishermen living in the village. There were some men, too, who lived on a neighbouring estate, and held land in Futtehpoor. There is no doubt that the Kachis originally settled on this spot and cleared the lands, but, in or before the last century, in an evil hour, they made some sort of compact for their own protection with the Canoongo of the pergunneh, which ended in his claiming the property. Any really good title he never had. However, his heirs found it easy to obtain a "*decree*" from our Civil Courts, soon after their first establishment, and the Kachis sunk for ever into the condition of cultivators.

From the Canoongo's family Runjeet bought the village. A young active man of the Kayath caste was just then the village accountant, by name Lulloo, with whom Runjeet easily made arrangements for the management of his new purchase. Runjeet was a fine, generous old man, and at once agreed that the Kachi cultivators should be allowed to hold their lands, as before, at easy rents. A rent-roll was drawn up and agreed to, which gave Runjeet, after the payment of all demands, a net profit of 400 rupees per annum. He led a very easy life, dwelling, as we said before, on his other property near the Ganges' bank. Twice a-year it was his custom to ride over to Futtehpoor, to spend a few days, and to collect, or rather to receive his rents. These half-yearly rent audits were at the period of the spring and autumnal harvests, when quite as many compliments passed between landlord and tenants as are customary on such occasions in Old England; and we are bound to say, quite as much good feeling was shown. Lulloo generally had the cash ready tied up in sundry little bundles, which were opened with a good many hints at the trouble he had undergone in the collection. Occasionally some wretched fisherman, or other low-caste tenant, was dragged up to account for a few rupees due on his little plot of ground, when Runjeet would look very black; but the matter was generally settled by some other tenants agreeing to give security for the debtor. One point of difference there is between Indian and English rent-days; instead of the landlord's giving a dinner to the tenants, the tenant generally makes some offering to the landlord. At least such was the custom at Futtehpoor. When Runjeet's old grey mare was seen coming down the slope near which the village lay, one man set off to the river to get some fish, another brought a little sugar and milk, a third ran for a bundle of grass or straw; in short, all hastened to welcome their "*malik*" with little offerings and many cries of "*Johar*,"* &c. Having eaten, drunk, slept, smoked, scolded, laughed, and chatted enough, the old man, after

* *Johar* is the salutation addressed by an inferior to a superior in the Central Doab, except, of course, to a Brahmin, who is addressed with "*Pai lugee*."

a few days' stay, put his money into his saddle-bags, primed his pistols (the same which he carried with Leek Sahib), and rode off home.

Runjeet's tenure of Futtehpoor is the simplest form of what is called zemindarree tenure. Its incidents are merely these: he must pay his revenue tax to Government, and he must collect from his tenants according to the rent-roll. If he failed in his engagements to the State, his rights as proprietor would be sold or farmed. If he tried to collect from his tenants more than was settled and entered in the rent-roll, they might rebel; though, at the period of which we write, they would not probably have succeeded in trying to oppose the will of a wealthy superior. We have no tenure in India simpler than this holding of Futtehpoor, except in the few cases of freeholds, or lands which pay no revenue to the State; and, even in these cases of freehold, the State claims the right to arbitrate between landlord and tenant. Zemindarree sole, in which a single proprietor enjoys the entire proprietary profit of an estate, exists generally in villages recently purchased, like Futtehpoor, or in the domains of some Rajahs or other large proprietors, in whose families the head succeeds to the undivided property in the land. In such a case as Futtehpoor, the simplicity of tenure will generally not last long. A few years passed pleasantly over Runjeet's head, when the old soldier became restless and ailing, and determined to go off on a pilgrimage to Gyah. He died on the way, leaving his estates to his two sons, Shere

Singh and Baz Singh, whose names were entered in the Government books in the room of their father's. The village accountant Lulloo went on collecting the rents as before, and paid the proceeds, after deducting the revenue dues and village expenses, to the two sons in equal proportions. This was the first step; Futtehpoor was now a partnership concern. As time passed on, the grandsons of Runjeet grew up, and about the year 1833 were six in number, viz.:

| *Sons of Shere Singh.* | *Sons of Baz Singh.* |
|---|---|
| Aman. | Soojan. |
| Koondun. | Putram. |
| Jeyt. | |
| Sooltan. | |

One or two unhealthy seasons passed, and the two elders, Shere Singh and Baz Singh, died. Their names were forthwith scratched off the collector's books, and those of their eldest sons, Aman and Soojan, were entered, who became henceforth, in village and cutcherry parlance, *Lumberdars* of the shares of their fathers, or, in other words, of *Puttee* Shere Singh and *Puttee* Baz Singh. When Lulloo came over from Futtehpoor with the rent, he used to present a scroll, which being deciphered, ran thus:—

ACCOUNT OF MOUZA FUTTEHPOOR.

EXAMPLE I.

| | *Rs.* | *As.* | *P.* |
|---|---|---|---|
| Proceeds in Cash .............. | 1200 | 0 | 0 |
| Paid for Revenue .............. | 700 | 0 | 0 |
| Paid for Village Expenses ...... | 100 | 0 | 0 |
| Balance being Profit .......... | 400 | 0 | 0 |

DISTRIBUTION OF PROFIT.

| Names of Sharers. | Extent of Share in Biswas. | Share of Profit. |
|---|---|---|
| Aman ............. | $2\frac{1}{2}$ | Rs........200 |
| Koondun ........ | $2\frac{1}{2}$ | |
| Jeyt ............ | $2\frac{1}{2}$ | |
| Sooltan .......... | $2\frac{1}{2}$ | |
| Soojan .......... | 5 | Rs........200 |
| Putram .......... | 5 | |
| | Total Rs........ | 400 |

Every estate consists of twenty imaginary Biswas, or one Beegha. These Biswas are again subdivided into Biswansis, and the Biswansi is further divided into Cutchwansis, and so on. Towards Bengal the imaginary division is calculated in parts of a rupee instead of a beegha. In Futtehpoor, Aman had a $2\frac{1}{2}$ Biswa share, Soojan had a 5 Biswa share; in other words, Aman had a right to one-eighth part of the profits, and his cousin Soojan had a right to one-fourth of the profits. In short, the division of an integral estate into Biswas or Anas is merely a contrivance for calculating the profits and loss thereon in the most familiar manner. With the aid of little bits of stick, or *kunkur*, for tallies, these fractional accounts are most earnestly made and jealously watched in a large coparcenary holding, amidst a chorus of disputes and protestations which baffles description. However, to return to our village, which as yet, with Lulloo's good offices, got on swimmingly. A sad misfortune, however, was hanging over the brotherhood. Runjeet's fancy in settling at Rajpoor had been particularly taken with a spot of land, well wooded and dry, which hung over the Ganges. In spite of the warnings of some of his neighbours, the old soldier determined to build a small mud fort on this promontory, and here his grandsons with their wives and young children lived. They had much of the village land under their own management, and were in prosperous case, when, one rainy season, the river took an adverse turn, and washed away their home and a great slice of the land of Rajpoor. The brethren with their wives, little ones, and cattle, fled to a hamlet near at hand, and saved as much of their household goods as they could. One of the children died, the locality was considered unlucky, and at last it was decided that Rajpoor, or what was left of it, should be let, and that the family party should migrate in a body to their property at Futtehpoor. They had gone through some hardship and trouble before they reached their new home; as often happens under such trials, with loss of property came loss of union and fellowship. The ladies of the family, if the truth must be told, were the chief causes of mischief. Shere Singh's two elder sons had married Chohan Thakorynes, poor and proud, who looked down with no concealed contempt upon their sisters-in-law of the humbler Toomur tribe. The Toomur women, who had married Jeyt and Sooltan, in their turn, when it became necessary to bustle about and make themselves useful, reproached the Chohan women for their fine-lady airs. The women soon set the brothers quarrelling, and the strife became constant and furious. The sons of

Baz Singh, who were hitherto prudent bachelors, did their best to reconcile the disputes of their cousins, but without much success. Division of rights, separation of the common interest, seemed inevitable. Hitherto, in happier days, the four brothers had eaten their mess of food, had shared their produce, cattle, and money together; but this natural and economical arrangement could last no longer. Separate houses were built and occupied. A council of proprietors was called, and with frowning brows and stormy looks the brothers came together, and met their cousins under the shade of the village peepul-tree. It was determined that the property of the four disputants (for no two of them could keep on good terms) should be divided; each sharer was to take by lot his quotum of the ploughs, bullocks, buffaloes, domestic utensils, &c., and (as opportunity offered) cultivate what land he might require. The sons of Baz Singh, like good and sensible men, kept together. They, too, set to work to cultivate. Some of the land of Futtehpoor was held, at this time, by tenants who resided in a distant village; these readily gave it up; some was taken by the brethren as the Kachi cultivators died; and, in short, our Rajpoots soon got as much of the land into occupation as they could well manage.

Hitherto we have had to do with non-resident proprietors, who drew a certain profit from an estate with the lands of which they had no direct concern. Now we come to a holding, in which part of the land is occupied by the proprietors themselves, and part is let out, as before, to tenants. We spare our readers all uncouth Indian terms, so far as we can, but must claim quarter for one little word. The land held by a resident proprietor, *in his own hands*, is called *seer*, and, as this word is short and expressive, we shall often use it hereafter. When our six Rajpoots had fairly settled themselves in Futtehpoor, and had taken into their hands more or less *seer* land, a new settlement of accounts became necessary.

Lulloo, the village accountant, had known little comfort since the brethren had come to Futtehpoor. The tenants paid him less respect than before; one of the proprietors had set longing eyes on two little pet pieces of land of his, which, somehow or other, had not found their way into the rent-roll; and, in short, Lulloo's occupation, if not gone, was decidedly in a declining state. But what distressed the old man most, was the fear of giving offence to any one of his six lords and masters. The Rajpoots have an ugly trick of giving a hostile accountant a knock on the head, and visions of drawn tulwars and iron-bound clubs would disturb poor Lulloo whenever his masters got angry with him or with each other; which, to tell the truth, was rather often. The accounts which he had now to prepare, amidst a storm of invective and an occasional ugly threat of being *sumjhaoed*,* drove him almost to despair. And, indeed, his

* This very expressive word, when used as a threat, answers to the English menace, "I'll teach you to do so and so;" and when used in anger is full of murderous meaning.

was no easy task, to teach reason and moderation to a set of high-spirited obstinate men, who were unwilling to be guided by either. Aman, the elder son of Shere Singh, wanted his brothers to pay down cash for the land they held, and when they demurred, proceeded to attach their crops. He actually placed two boys and an old woman with a long stick at three corners of one of Sooltan's fields, when his proceedings were stopped by a cry of "*Már, már,*" and a sally from Sooltan, Koondun, and Jeyt, who threatened, not only to submerge Aman's watchers in the river, but to give their employer his *quietus* too. There was much shouting, and, as Aman's part was taken by the village watchmen and others, things looked ripe for a general action; when peace was restored by Lulloo, who, having placed first his turban and then his head at Aman's feet, and invoked the manes of old Runjeet, produced his budget, with the following deprecatory address.

"Why should the noble maliks, thakoors, and descendants of warriors, dispute like persons of low caste? Your prosperity is so great that you have plenty of land and nothing to pay. Let your servant explain. In this bag, as I told you before, are one hundred rupees, being the rents of the fields of your cultivators. The payments for the Government tax, for the expenses of the village, the watchman, and your humble servant, have been made. All that you have to do is to divide this money amongst you in its just proportions, like gentlemen; but, instead of that, you begin to fight like a set of ——" *Chumars,* he would have added, if he dared, but his voice was drowned in a general shout of applause. Hereupon Lulloo threw down his bag, and pulled out of a hollow bamboo a scroll, which, being interpreted, ran thus :—

EXAMPLE II.

| Name of Proprietor. | Profit on his Share. | Deduct Value of Seer. | Balance due to each. | Balance due from each. |
|---|---|---|---|---|
| Aman .... | Rs. 50 | 50 | 0 | 0 |
| Koondun .. | 50 | 35 | 15 | 0 |
| Jeyt ...... | 50 | 30 | 20 | 0 |
| Sooltan .... | 50 | 75 | 0 | 25 |
| Soojan with Putram | 200 | 110 | 90 | |

It will be observed that Sooltan, who had a large proportion of *seer,* had to put down 25 rupees, being the rent of land which he held in excess of his share of the profits (which are assumed at 400 rupees). This sum of 25 rupees, added to the 100 rupees of common rents from Lulloo's bag, was applied to make up to each proprietor his full share of the profits, as here shown. All payments for revenue, &c. had been made from the land held by common tenants. Thus, for the time being, peace was restored by Lulloo with his rupees and arithmetic.

A year or two later, the proprietors had taken a greater quantity of *seer* land into cultivation, the rent of which, at the existing rates, was as much as 600 rupees. Henceforth evidently a part of the revenue must be paid by them, for the land held by the common tenants no longer sufficed to meet all demands. Accordingly the elder sons of each family, Aman and Soojan, set to work as *lumberdars,* or head men, of *Puttee* Shere Singh and *Puttee* Baz Singh, to collect the money due from each share. When the revenue and village expenses had been paid, the accounts of the head men were produced for audit in the idle month of Jeyth, in the following form :—

EXAMPLE III.

| Names of Cultivators. | Area of Land in Beeghas. | Rent in Rupees. | Receipts. | Balances. |
|---|---|---|---|---|
| Aman ........ | 100 | 100 | 100 | 0 |
| Koondun ...... | 60 | 70 | 70 | 0 |
| Jeyt .......... | 40 | 60 | 60 | 0 |
| Sooltan........ | 140 | 150 | 140 | 10 |
| Soojan with Putram ........ | 200 | 220 | 220 | 0 |
| Other cultivators not proprietors | 530 | 590 | 490 | 0 |
| Sewaee Singhara | 0 | 10 | 10 | 0* |
| Total.... | 1070 | 1200 | 1190 | 10 |

The result of operations was further shown by a memorandum, thus :—

| Names of Sharers. | Amount of Share in Biswas. | Profit in Rupees. |
|---|---|---|
| Aman ............ | $2\frac{1}{2}$ | 50 |
| Koondun .......... | $2\frac{1}{2}$ | 50 |
| Jeyt .......... .. | $2\frac{1}{2}$ | 50 |
| Sooltan............ | $2\frac{1}{2}$ | 50 |
| Soojan with Putram.. | 10 | 200 |
| | 20 | Rs. .. 400 |

* Sewaee Singhara—Sewaee items of revenue are those generally manorial perquisites which the proprietor gets besides land rent, such as from fisheries, the Singhara root grown in pools, &c. &c.

The proceeds in this case have been taken to amount to 1200 rupees, of which 700 rupees go to Government revenue, and 100 rupees for village expenses, as in a former example. The remaining 400 rupees, after making every proprietor account for the rent of his *seer*, just like any other cultivator, will be distributed amongst the sharers as before, in proportion to the share of each.

About this time fortune smiled upon the brotherhood. The long-talked-of settlement (under Reg. ix. 1833) was in progress, and was extended to Futtehpoor. It was not thought necessary to raise the Government demand. But, as a general revision of rents was going on, the Rajpoots took the opportunity for raising their rent-roll. They determined to make the Kachis pay as much as the other tenants; and as their lands were productive, well tilled, and at low rents, the Kachis were unable to resist the advance. The increased profit which resulted from this measure, and from the letting of some fisheries advantageously, amounted in round numbers to 300 rupees. Old Lulloo, in a new turban, which had been given him on the occasion, making his reverence to the assembled brotherhood, thus spoke,—

"It is by your good fortune that the rent-roll, which your servant has with so much pains prepared, has been passed by the collector (may his prosperity be lasting!). Henceforth you will live on your lands, as becomes men of your birth, upon easy terms. The Kachis, who are accustomed to heat and labour, will pay the full rents which they ought to have paid long ago; you, the lords of the soil, instead of paying, as hitherto, like common cultivators, shall pay a light rent." The result of the new settlement was shortly this. The brethren held as much *seer* land as before, but, instead of paying the ordinary rents levied on other cultivators, they were henceforth to hold their land on *favoured* rates, indeed on nearly one half of what they had paid before. But, as we have observed, the seer held by each proprietor in Futtehpoor had depended on the means of the several brothers, and was not in proportion to the share of each in the whole estate. It was necessary, therefore, in the annual settlement of accounts, to retain the form shown in Example 3. Every proprietor was first charged at the usual high rate of rent on his seer, and the only difference was, that, instead of distributing 400 rupees of profit, 700 rupees were divided. It may, perhaps, be here asked, what was the use of lowering the seer-land rate? The answer is, that the proprietors thereby concealed, as far as they could, the real money value of the proceeds from the estate, and, by showing a low and poor rent-roll, conceived that they made out a better claim to raise the rents of the Kachi cultivators. We have heard of men, by no means wanting in sagacity, who have been sorely puzzled by this plan of favoured rates. They found a village doing apparently very well with a rent-roll on paper which nobody disputed, yet actually giving a total sum less than the Government revenue. They did not know that perhaps half the land, and the best land too, was entered at rent-rates only one half of the real value.

But we must hasten on with our village history. It does not appear that the comparative prosperity of the brethren put a stop to their disputes. Aman, the elder brother, became very unpopular with the others of his family. It fell to him as *lumberdar*, or head man, with his cousin Soojan, to collect the rents from the common tenants, and to disburse the public money. His younger brothers suspected that he made money by his office at their expense. At last nothing would satisfy them but a division of the tenants, which was made by the process called *assamee bhant* in the following manner:— *First*, A schedule was drawn up by old Lulloo, showing the name and caste of every cultivator having no proprietary rights, his quotum of rent, extent of land, and so on, with grand totals of rent and land. *Secondly*, Two scrolls were prepared, in which an equal amount of rental was entered. Aman and Soojan drew each by lot one of these scrolls, and took the tenants entered in their respective lots. Thus the common tenant land was divided between the two Puttees of Shere Singh and Baz Singh. *Thirdly*. The lot drawn by Aman was subdivided into four lists, which were drawn by lot by the four brothers. This process may seem simple enough on paper, but as a sort of *catalogue raisonné* of tenants had been made out, it was a tedious business. The solvency, caste, habits, and character of each tenant, and all such points, were as closely canvassed as those of a horse by a Yorkshire jockey. Two months of incessant talking and wrangling left poor Lulloo worn out and exhausted, and he soon after died, leaving as a legacy the following memorandum :—

ASSAMEEWAR KHEWUT, OR DIVISION OF TENANTS, OF THE VILLAGE FUTTEHPOOR.

EXAMPLE IV.

| Name of Puttee. | Name of Sharer. | Names of Tenants. | Extent of Tenant Land in Beeghas. | Rent in Rupees. |
|---|---|---|---|---|
| Shere Singh | Aman .. | Budloo, &c. | 50 | 100 |
| | Koondun | Nunkoo, &c. | 60 | 100 |
| | Jeyt .... | Khedoo, &c. | 50 | 100 |
| | Sooltan | Bowannee, &c. | 80 | 100 |
| Bah Singh | | | | |
| | Soojan with Putram.. | Bikhee, &c. &c. | 240 | 400 |

It now was the duty of each of Shere Singh's sons to collect from his own tenants, according to this list. The *seer* land accounts were kept as before. The advantage of this arrangement was, that one brother could not accuse the other of pocketing the rents.

As time passed on, the good management of the *united* brethren, Soojan and Putram, had its due effect; their tenants were flourishing, whilst those of the four brothers were decaying. The sons of Shere Singh declared that the sons of Baz Singh had all the good fields, and demanded a distribution of the cultivated land. The six proprietors assembled in solemn conclave, and agreed to leave it to the elder brother of each family, *i. e.* to the two *lumberdars*, to divide the cultivation, which was accordingly apportioned in equal lots to the two families, leaving only a certain remnant of waste land, jungle, and some small freeholds of the village Brahmin, in common. An application was made to the collector of the district for leave to file a new statement of liabilities: thus the village of Futtehpoor was transferred from the list of "zemindarree" estates to that of estates held in "imperfect putteedaree" tenure. Henceforth the sons of Shere Singh paid a separate share (the half) of the Government revenue; their cousins, the sons of Baz Singh, paid the other half. If a balance occurred in one division of the estate, the revenue authorities came, in the first instance, down upon the defaulting division; if the defaulters did not pay what was due from them, their lands were offered in farm to the proprietors of the solvent division, who were expected for that consideration to discharge the debt. Failing in this obligation, to which from the constitution of the holding they were liable, Government would hold the entire estate responsible, and would proceed against it by farm or sale, as might be expedient. But the proprietors might, if they chose, set themselves free from the degree of joint responsibility which attached to their position, by claiming a full and entire legal separation. When such a separation takes place in Futtehpoor, as will be the case some day, the two separate holdings will be entered in the Government books as two distinct estates; one will be called Futtehpoor Shere Singh, the other Futtehpoor Baz Singh, and the original relationship will be lost and gone.

Such, then, is the progress of village affairs, by which the simple "zemindarree" tenure is every day tending towards the various complications of "imperfect putteedaree;" or, in other words, from sole or coparcenary tenure towards tenure in severalty. So, again, the imperfect severalty gradually merges into a complete and perfect division of estates.*

We have traced, at the risk of our readers' patience, the fortunes of an Indian village community. Before attempting to show the effect upon such a body which our reformed revenue laws may produce, let us glance at the condition of these corporations under the Mahometan emperors. Akber's enlightened policy did much to prevent them from State oppression; but taking them at their best, in

* It is not easy to foresee what will be the effect on the people of the extreme subdivision of estates which must in time take place. The right to claim such a division recommends itself at once to every English mind, and its attendant inconveniences are to be traced to the original law of equal inheritance, and not to the respect which we have shown to the rights of private property. We must not judge of the political effect of the subdivision of landed property from what we see in European countries. Its *probable* result is the converse of what we observe, for instance, in France; *there* a hot spirit of enterprise, vanity, and personal ambition, tempts the petty owner from the plough and from the country to join the masses of the cities; his pride is not in his vineyard or corn-field, but in "la belle France," and in her municipal institutions, in which he hopes some day to figure. Now, in India, it is needless to say that a division of the large brotherhoods, whether desirable or not for other reasons, can politically only tend to peace and subordination.

his time, it is certain that the relative rights of sharers never received the attention which they deserved. The history of our large village clans, from the days of Akber downwards, is one tale of discord and oppression. Village rights were recognised then in the Doab about as much as they are now in Oude; the claims of equal inheritance were acknowledged in theory, but denied in practice, and might made right. Later still, the most arbitrary and oppressive means were taken by the Government, or by the Talookdars, and others to whom the Government delegated its authority, to squeeze the revenue out of the people. Insolvent zemindars were beaten, fed upon salt, placed up to the armpits in ordure, their children taken in pledge; in short, were tortured in every way that cruelty and avarice might suggest. This was the lot of the weak; the powerful took to their forts, and when starved out of them, to their jungles, and defied the Government altogether. As for justice between man and man, sharer and sharer, it was not thought of. Such was the state of things in the Doab when Lord Wellesley first occupied it, and twenty years later matters were not much improved; there was, perhaps, less fighting, but more injustice. Indeed, even up to the time of the present settlement under Reg. ix. 1833, the manner of collecting the revenue was most unjust and irregular. The innocent and the guilty (of revenue default) met one common ruin. To give one instance: a village held by sharers where lands were divided, and who were justly liable, each for their own quotum of revenue, fell into balance, owing to the rascality of some of the sharers, who chose to live at the expense of their brethren. The collector, instead of coming down upon the defaulter, would pass the order, common under the *ancien régime*,—"Let *Bilah-bundee* be made." What does the reader suppose *Bilah-bundee* means? So far as we can learn its etymology, it means a stopping of holes; and in its original vernacular use, it applies to the stopping a fox or a rat into his hole. When applied to Indian bipeds, *Bilah-bundee* means a stopping of all those vents through which the coin of the proprietors of a village might otherwise ooze out, to the detriment of the Government revenue. When this process was ordered, off went the Tehsildar with his followers, and laid the best men of the village by the heels. Every decent householder of the proprietary family was kept in durance until the money wanted was paid up. If A paid for B, or C for D, it mattered not; the revenue was realised, and the collector was satisfied.

"Delirant reges, plectuntur Achivi!"

By such harsh measures as this, by *káfee záminee** and other contrivances, was the revenue

* Káfee záminee, or sufficient security. The Tehsildar was, in the days of which we are writing, told to take káfee záminee, or full security. Some powerful hanger-on of the Tehsildaree cutcherry undertook to give this security, and then proceeded to levy the money due in the most harassing and arbitrary manner, until the defaulter had to buy him off by a payment much greater than the original debt due on the revenue account.

taken.* There are districts which to this day have not entirely recovered from the withering rule of some of our early collectors.

Blessings be upon the good men and true who came to the rescue of the Indian village communities. It was not their lot, nor perhaps their ambition, to accomplish what may be called an European reputation; but their names will here live in the grateful memory of millions. Amongst these our revenue reformers stands Robert Bird pre-eminent. Gifted with a clear head and a firm hand, a cultivated mind and determined will, he it was who first applied a complete remedy to the injuries of the landed proprietors. Him might the revenue student of the present day apostrophise in the glowing terms once applied to the master of a far different philosophy,—

> " E tenebris tantis tam clarum extollere lumen
> Qui primus potuisti, illustrans commoda vitæ,
> Te sequor."

It was no selfish spirit, no desire to grasp at the resources of the country, which gave impulse to Bird's inquiries; the *animus* at work was, in the first instance, purely a judicial one. It had been

* These short, simple, and summary ways of getting money out of the people, live in the fond remembrance of many a grey-headed native revenue official. Ask such an one how it is that now-a-days, though the revenue has been perhaps lowered, every man's right defined, every man's quotum settled, the money does not come in to the day as it did in the *good* old times. "Ah, sir," he will reply, " in those days we went to work like men, and took the money; now you sit like beggars and

his lot as judge of a district to note the cruel grievances and endless entanglements of affairs caused by our early revenue and civil procedure. Professing to govern according to the law and constitution of the people, our best intentions had ended only in their damage and disappointment. Mr. Bird longed to see a practice introduced more consistent with our principles. The "painful and disinterested researches of a judicial officer into the best mode of obviating the difficulties and promoting the welfare of the landed interest of the country:" these are, in his own words, the motives and proceedings which led to our great revenue reforms. The movement was more than disinterested; it was dictated by a spirit of the most active philanthropy. Like most generous actions, it brought its own reward; for again, to use Bird's language, "the same methods of procedure which were best calculated to determine the rights of individuals were also found to be most conducive to the ascertainment of such an equal and moderate revenue demand as is most for the interest of the State." It is not our intention to follow out the details of the survey and settlement proceedings which formed the basis of our existing revenue code. It will suf-

ask for it. We had then bilah-bundee, káfee záminee; or, if that would not do, we tied a defaulter up on the nearest tree, and let him down when his wife brought the money. Now you are more like bankers than revenue officers; but there is nothing like a little compulsion. *Seedhee oonglee se ghee nuheen nikalta.* You can't take butter up without closing your fingers. Village people won't pay unless they are constrained."

fice to draw attention to the spirit which has pervaded this great work. We have shown that in every village there is a rule, more or less known, and varying according to circumstances, but still a rule, whereby the distribution of property in the land should be enforced. This rule, full of meaning, and fitted to the habits of the people, is to them what the common law is to us. A *lex scripta* had been brought in, which knew not and heeded not the voice of ages. It was Bird's duty, and one which he skilfully executed, to take up the broken links of the village common law, and to fling aside or amend such of our statutes as could not be brought to agreement with it. His it was to introduce a general and scientific survey of the country, to mark carefully and to record the boundaries of every village, to register the separate possessions, rights, privileges and responsibilities of those communities who held their lands in severalty, and of the several interests of those who held land in common.

Any of our readers who may have taken the trouble to follow the various forms of village management given in these notes, will at once see how all-important it must be to the village proprietors that their holdings be fully recognised and understood by the revenue authorities. A process, which under one form of village rule is legitimate and appropriate, may be under another form disastrous. Not to multiply examples which might be tedious, let us take one instance. Suppose that in the village Futtehpoor, after the division of the land between the two families, default occurred in Puttee Shere Singh, *i. e.* the share held by the four brothers. According to the old system, or rather no system, the Tehsildar would have laid hold of all the sharers: he knew and cared nothing about the village law and constitution, and the sons of Baz Singh would have had to pay for the default of their cousins—the innocent for the guilty. By the present rules, the four brothers would be called to account for their own debts. They know this, and therefore strive to keep their accounts clear; but formerly, when the idle or dissolute and the industrious met one common fate, what inducement had any man to honest exertion? *Formerly* sales of land, which swept away the rights of whole families, involving the frugal and the careless in one ruin, farms which destroyed the life and spirit of entire tribes of men, were of almost daily occurrence. *Now* it is impossible for a collector to apply any of the more stringent processes for securing the revenue, without giving clear and sufficient reasons for his proceedings. The rights of landed proprietors are watched with a jealousy that astonishes even themselves. No petty owner of twenty acres can have his holding transferred for a few years on account of revenue default, without the sanction and scrutiny of the head of the local Government. The danger is now, not that matters will be done illegally or informally, but that the revenue officers will become too much tied to forms and observances. They must beware of degenerating into men of mere red-tape routine. To support a career of much drudgery and self-denial, they require a strong infusion of life into their work, and a touch of enthusiasm. For them, a mere cold discharge of duty will hardly suffice; they should encourage, also, a hearty affection for the people.

How mysterious is the Providence which has placed a handful of English gentlemen at the head of Indian affairs! Never let it be said that they have neglected the wonderful opportunities of their destiny. The duties of the English in India are to the people. The more an officer of the Government can mix with them the better. Let him know them thoroughly; to do this he need only listen to them patiently. They are prone to confide in the justice and kindness of their European masters. That they are incapable of feeling or of gratitude is false. His must be a cold heart and barren imagination that cannot respond to the feelings with which our Indian subjects regard their village homes—homes which to their simple minds are little worlds of history and romance, as well as of common life. With some kindred feeling will they revere the man of power who will take the pains to do them justice, and will not refuse them sympathy. Nor is it only in its moral aspect that official life in India may please. We allow the physical privations and sufferings of cutcherry work in the hot season to be severe; but when the sun gives some respite, there are many enjoyments in store for the man of simple tastes and contented mind. Then is the time to sally out into the fields amongst the people. Amidst their pleasant villages, under the shade of the tent, or the well-grown mango grove, the wanderer may almost forget that he is in a strange land. India need not, and cannot rival England in our affections. We miss the hill and dale, the steaming pasture, the clear trout stream of our native land; but still we may rejoice in the rural beauties of a less favoured scene. The freshness of an Indian morning in the cooler season may charm us, if only by contrast. 'Tis true we do not wake to the carol of the thrush, nor to the voice of "newly-wakened herds" lowing across the meadow; our dreams are not mixed up with the sound of the gardener's early scythe under our window; yet still we wake to a glorious morn. The air is clear and frosty; the dew glistens on the broad fields of springing wheat and barley; all nature seems instinct with life and joy. A mixed sound, the shouts of the villagers driving out their cattle to the field, the barking of their dogs, the shrill voices of their children, come sweeping down the morning breeze; nearer still is a chorus of birds, amidst which the silvery note of the dove rises ever clear and long. Man and horse seem alike inspirited by the fresh breath of the morning, as we gallop along, throwing "*atra cura*" to the winds. If there be any country in which Nature never smiles to win poor man away from his cares, it is not India. Mornings passed in exercise or rural sport, days under the trees or in the cheerful tent, the village people all around to claim our care and protection; time thus spent flies fast and well. If home and home scenes linger in the memories of the Englishman in India, it is well ; but well, too, if he remember how valuable the passing hour may be. Each day may see some old feud reconciled, some village strife composed, some benefit conferred upon a grateful people. And if the official man look forward to a time when he may hope once more to be at home, and amidst the enjoyments of private life, how pleasant is the hope that he may even then live in the regard of a wild yet noble race, who love his memory, because he felt for them and tried to do them good.

# IV.

## CASE OF THE NON-PROPRIETARY CULTIVATING CLASSES.

"*L'auteur de l'institution est demeuré inconnu.*" Thus does the Baron Barchou de Penhoën end his learned disquisition on the village republics of the East.* Monsieur le Baron is quite right; nobody knows who was the author of the Indian village institution; and for a very sufficient reason, at all events, so far as our north-western provinces are concerned; for they never had any living author. The Indian village system in the north-west cannot justly be called an *institution* at all; it is just a *status*, growing out of peculiar circumstances, and existing because of its obedience to those circumstances. Its author is *necessity*, that fruitful mother of invention, and the secret of its growth and stability is to be found in its powers of assimilation to her rough nutriment and self-adaptation to her

* "L'Inde sous la Domination Anglaise, par le Baron Barchou de Penhoën." Paris, 1844.

stern decrees. The Indian village struggles on amidst outward violence and inward convulsion, not by virtue of any refined and complex economy, but thanks to certain elastic and long-living qualities, which in the social as well as in the animal world consist best with a low degree of organisation. Philosophers may dream about the "force of organisation," which has withstood "historical boule-versements" and "political cataclysms;"*—for our parts, we believe it is just the absence of any artificial organisation that has kept our village system alive. The agricultural communities form the polypi of the social world, the link between living and mere vegetating organisation; their peculiarity is that they can survive anything. Cut them in pieces, disperse or batter them, they still go on living, and prosper not the less. And thus it is that, whilst kings, empires, and dynasties, have passed away, the humble village community remains.

It does not follow that, because the village system is simple, there has been any lack of honest wit in its growth and developement. The fact is, that our early village worthies, though the children rather than the parents of the constitution to which they belonged, were long-headed and wary politicians. Like cautious seamen in rough weather, whose chief care is to keep their craft well to the wind, they preferred security to progress. There is an honest policy running through all their proceedings which

* "L'Inde sous la Domination," &c., vol. i. chap. iv. p. 66.

we cannot help admiring, and to which we would gladly draw the attention of our readers.

A village, so called in the revenue parlance of the north-western provinces, is a tract of land with fixed name and boundaries, whether it contain what in England is properly called a village or not. It may be inhabited, or it may be *be-churagh* (without a lamp), as those estates are called which contain no human habitation; it may contain one cluster of houses, or many. When the sturdy *coloni* from the far North had taken their stand in the country, the land gradually became parcelled out amongst the settlers. The forests fell before increasing numbers, and branches from each parent stock peopled hamlets on every side. The country became dotted with fort-like homesteads, each homestead with its little oasis of cultured land, and with its herds and flocks grazing in the farther jungle. Centuries passed away: time after time the Mahometan tents whitened new fields of conquest; India bowed and fell before the fierce sons of the Prophet; but the Indian village system stood unhurt. The people surrendered their political rights; but it was only to cling more closely to their social and domestic institutions. If the truth must be told, the patriotism of our Indian "village Hampdens" is of a somewhat contracted nature; like the Vicar of Bray, so long as they get their share of the loaves and fishes, they care very little who may be the dispenser thereof. It suited the earlier Mahometans to treat their new subjects well. As time rolled on, the Emperor Akber came, and India's Doomsday

Book was compiled. Every village was enrolled in the imperial register; the name of its dependent hamlets, and the amount of its tribute, were fairly entered; and that distribution of landed property into *mehals* or estates, which had so long existed, and which still exists, was recorded in imperishable characters. To this day, or at all events up to the period of the late great settlement, the books of Akber were consulted in cases affecting landed property, and the revenue forms and terms then introduced are still known amongst us. Akber was the friend of the village communities, who, under his vigorous yet paternal rule, had little to desire. They had lost what they little prized, national superiority; they held fast what they dearly valued, family union and stability. When worse days came, their foes were of their own household; and such of the communities as lost their independence, fell rather by the treachery of their own members than by any foreign violence. The chiefs who enslaved them were of their own flesh and blood.

Under these varied fortunes, then, it was that the simple patriarchal form of village government flourished. The heads of each large family or tribe, assisted by the common voice of the brotherhood, held undisputed sway, each in their own domain. Feuds or differences were settled by the members of the village council (or *punchayet*), sitting, not as judges, but as arbitrators between man and man, and carrying out their awards rather by the force of opinion than by the actual arm of the law. To the minds of men in this simple state, the *vox populi* is indeed the *vox Dei*, and men who would yield to nothing else, would yet listen to the voice of the majority; for, however he might despise law, no Indian yet ever quite despised public opinion.

So far, then, as the regulation of landed property is concerned, there is a common law well known and dear to the people. Happily for them and for us, our revenue legislators have become aware of this, and have at last enlisted the sympathies of the people in their favour, simply by acting in accordance with those sympathies rather than in spite of them. We say, happily; for one thing is certain, if we would rule the people of India well and wisely, we must rule them in their own way. Legal fictions, John Roes and Richard Does, may suit John Bull (though even he is getting rather restive under them), but they will not do here. "I have tried everything," said a young magistrate to William Frazer, the lamented Commissioner of Delhi, "I have imprisoned, fined, and taken security from the people of —— pergunneh, but I can't keep them quiet." "Did you ever try," asked Frazer, "to *let them alone?*" Now, this is just the treatment which the Indian village system requires, *to be let alone*. A policy which has stood for twelve centuries, whilst half-a-dozen governments have tumbled into the dust, will outlive anything except needless and officious interference. For us to set to work to improve or alter these institutions, would be about as wise as it would be for the native Indian communities to attempt to regulate the British constitution. The one and the other are alike the offspring of circumstances, rather than of design, and both should be left to work out unaided and unfettered the part which Providence has assigned to them.

It is obvious, that in societies such as we have been describing, where union is strength, unity must at all events be maintained. But, as division of interest enters more or less into all human affairs, the question soon arose, How can general union be made best to consist with individual freedom and independence? It happens that the idiosyncracy of the Indian agriculturist was well suited to the solving of this problem. His was not an astute mind clinging with sophisticated tenacity to his own rights, and careless of carrying the affections of others along with him; nor yet, on the other hand, was his a soft-yielding nature to give himself blindly up to the leading of other men. His character was a compound of self-will and unselfishness. Let us see with how much strong sense and sound mother-wit he could act when occasion required it. We will take for an example this very matter of dividing the land. But, first, we must ask our readers whether they ever walked through a Derbyshire pottery. If so, they may remember that a day's work of a pottery-turner is reckoned at so many dozens. Now dishes and plates are counted twelve to a dozen; but when you come to jugs, you will find one gigantic fellow set down as a dozen, while thirty-six little jugs, equal in value to the single monster, will be put down as a dozen also. This plan is adopted in order to keep up a uniformity of prices in the accounts.* As a mere counting-house transaction, there is nothing very remarkable in this; but its coincidence with an arrangement many centuries old in India for the division of the land is curious. Most Indian villages contain three or more kinds of land, well known to the people, and appreciated by them. These divisions may have reference to the nature of the soil, the facilities of irrigation, or to the relative position of the land to the village. Let us suppose this last division, when the land will be estimated thus:—

First.—The land close to the homestead.

Second.—The middle circle of land.

Third.—The outer circle.†

The first quality being well manured and easily watched and watered, is the most valuable. The second quality of land is farther a-field, has fewer advantages, and a less value. The third quality of land, remote from the village, is still less valuable. Now, when a proprietor of land claims a separation of his share, he may naturally expect to have a slice of each quality of land. If poor land be given him, he will require that the deficiency in quality be made up in quantity. A valuation and appraisement such as must be made is obviously a work of complication and difficulty, even supposing all

* See Chambers' "Edinburgh Journal," Nov. 1848, for a good description of this mode of keeping accounts.

† The first is called *Barah*, *Gohūnee*, *Goonduh*.

The second, *Munjha*, *Manj*.

The third, *Burhar* or *Har*. In the Benares province, these circles are called, 1st, *Goindh*; 2d, *Bichkur*; and 3d, *Palo*.

parties to be desirous to act fairly and cordially; but, amongst a set of violent and suspicious men, the difficulty and delay of the process becomes increased indefinitely. To remedy this evil, some long-headed patriarch devised the very scheme which we have described as prevailing at the Derbyshire potteries. Like the pottery masters with their imaginary dozens, the villagers set up a standard measure of imaginary *begahs*, and divide the estate accordingly. In the Central Doab there is a word in use, *touzee*, or *towjee* as the rustics pronounce it, which signifies a division, a separate part. From this word the village imaginary begah was named a *touzee begah*, because it was the begah or land-measure used for making a division of the land. An estate was divided into several (say a hundred) of these imaginary begahs. The relative value of each of the three (or more) sorts of soil was set down—for instance, one *towjee begah* was declared equal to four ordinary begahs of land of the first quality—to six ordinary begahs of land of the second quality—or to eight begahs of the land of the third quality. It was then ruled by common consent, that the shares of the brethren should be computed henceforth in *towjee begahs*. In future the sharers, instead of claiming so many *biswas* or *anas*—*i. e.* so many fractions of a begah or of a rupee, would state their rights in *towjee begahs*. The result of this was, that when a division was claimed, it remained with the village to apportion off just what land was most convenient to spare to the claimant. He could not demand, as he might have done but for the custom of *towjee bhaut,* a slice of the best land, or of each sort, a bit of each field, or of every hamlet; all he could claim was so many *towjee begahs,* and those he would get in whatever shape was most convenient to the community at large. This custom tended to check capricious men from demanding a separation of the land on insufficient cause, and helped to prevent disputes and keep the brethren together. It had the disadvantage of being too artificial to last amidst all the reverses of fortune to which the village communities were liable, and, though once widely prevailing, is now seldom found. We have detailed this little trait of village policy to show what the village genius is, how capable of simple yet effectual expedients for successful self-management.

So far we have tried in our "Notes" to give some account of the landed proprietors in the north-western provinces, of their rise, progress, and policy, whether domestic or social. Now, though an Indian landed proprietor may be, and is, a very different kind of animal from his European congener, the man of old oaks, elms, and park-gates, he has still in his own way very considerable *landed* duties, rights, and dignities. We have already said that he forms one of a lordly brotherhood, not the mere member of a corporation. He has no equals in the village, save those of his own tribe. Lord of the soil, his authority is paramount; and the other village officers, such as the accountant or watchman, are virtually his servants. But in most estates we shall find, besides the superior proprietors, a large and important agricultural class of persons, who hold lands by an inferior title in tenant-right. Every one knows that in India all sorts of offices and occupations descend from father to son, almost by right. Hereditary cultivators are just as common as hereditary barbers, washermen, or carpenters. It would require more time and learning than we can command to define how these cultivating non-proprietary classes were regarded by former governments. We have our own impressions on the subject, and they lead us to believe that the merely cultivating tribes, whose ploughshare was not readily convertible into a sword, met with very scurvy treatment under the Mahometan rule; and we see reason to suppose that they were generally considered as mere "hewers of wood and drawers of water," the Helots of the agricultural classes. The British Government early found the difficulty of drawing a line between these hereditary cultivators and the more depressed of the proprietary classes; and no wonder, for many cultivators were proprietors, and many proprietors were cultivators. Hence, we may trace in our early revenue laws an evident anxiety to protect the tenant classes, mixed with considerable doubt and hesitation as to how far they ought to be protected. It was and is a difficult subject to deal with, for if the mere cultivators are made independent of the proprietor, the superior holder is placed in a false position; he has the responsibilities of a land-owner without the power. On the other hand, if the cultivators are made mere tenants at will, a most important body of men, the very sinews of the state, are crushed. We are treating the matter as one of policy. It is not easy to argue the abstract justice of the case until we obtain clearer light than has yet been thrown on the origin and on the condition of the tenant classes under former Governments. On the whole, it is probable that policy and justice go together in this, as in other cases; and we are disposed to stand up for the tenant-right. Some protection must be given to this useful and industrious class. We do not find many Dukes of Devonshire or Bedford amongst our eastern landlords, who, to tell the truth, are much more likely to kick a tenant out of his mud hut than to build a villa or model-cottage for him. Besides all this, the Government, as lord paramount, has a hold over the landed proprietors, and can justly demand that the ancient hereditary cultivator shall not be disturbed so long as he pays his rent. Some such provision was ostensibly made by former Governments; and we are right to protect and encourage in every legal manner the peasantry of the country. Nor are they slow to learn and appreciate the privileges of their position. In most districts, the collector on his daily journey to cutcherry is followed by cultivators, with petitions in their hands, calling upon him to settle their disputes with the proprietors of the land. One man has a bunch of green corn or of young trees, which have been forcibly plucked up by some domineering landlord, and which are prominently displayed "*ad miseri-*

*cordiam*" to the district chief; before the cutcherry stands a group of men with their ploughs and oxen, intended to catch the eye of the functionary, and to show how the owners have been ejected from their land. For one hour that the Revenue Collector spends in securing the Government revenue, he and his numerous subordinates spend six hours in the service of the people, and particularly in arbitrating between landlord and tenant. The expositions of the law in such cases, put forth authoritatively by the Government of late years, throw as much light as possible on a somewhat obscure subject. The commentary is better than the text, for the law itself between landlord and tenant is, however copious, neither clear nor explicit.

We should be glad to see a short stringent Act to define the rights of the zemindar and the ryot—*Anglicè*, the landlord and tenant. A very few words might settle questions which now give anxiety and uncertainty to the proprietors, as well as the under-tenants of the land. We may just mention, for example, difficulties which may occur under existing rules. What period of time gives a tenant a prescriptive right of tenancy? * Under

* The terms in use to denote cultivators possessed of tenant-rights are as various as the customs by which the extent of these rights are estimated. They are sometimes called *mouroosi*, or hereditary; *chupperbund*, or householders; *kudcem*, or ancient; cultivators from other villages are called *paikasht*. Under existing rules, they cannot be summarily dispossessed by the proprietor of the land, any more than the resident ryots. We have to remark of all this class that they have no power to sell, or, under ordinary circumstances, to transfer their interest in

what circumstances can a landlord raise his rents? What remedy can a landlord take against an impracticable tenant, who allows the land to become deteriorated by neglect? Can a tenant, under any circumstances, transfer his rights to another; for instance, if he go on a pilgrimage, or be afflicted with an incurable disease?* Hitherto, (we speak of the upper provinces), questions of this nature have easily settled themselves, because tenants have been in demand, and the landlords would as readily have parted with their cattle as with their ryots. But now we are on the eve of great changes;—the population, cut short by the years of famine in 1837 and 1838, is rapidly recovering itself, and we shall soon have the great canal forming a second valley of the Ganges, down the back-bone of the Doab. Every day the value of the tenant-right is increasing, the landlord watches the rising families of tenants with un-

the land to another; but on the demise of a tenant cultivator, his nearest heir succeeds.

* We are not aware that it has ever been ruled by sufficient authority, what is the longest period that may elapse (short, of course, of a year) between the date of a cultivator's ejectment by a landlord from his holding, and the date at which a petition for redress must be filed in the summary suit department. As it is, tenants often wait to see what the season promises to be; and if they see no sign of rain, hold themselves in readiness to resist all demands for rent. If the landlord makes his own arrangements for tilling the tenant's former holding, and then, late in the season, a good fall of rain comes, the tenants rush in to the collector to complain of ouster. To prevent this, different rules prevail in different places. In this, as in other cases, one uniform mode of procedure is desirable.

mixed pride no longer, but begins to feel jealous of every man who absorbs a part of the profits of the land.

We have said this much about the tenant-right, without saying who these tenants are. To tell the truth, the ethnography of the tribes of Hindoo cultivators has puzzled wiser heads than ours.

So far as we can learn, the lower tribes sprang from *mésalliances* between the members of the higher ones. In many villages, those who are now mere cultivators under a superior proprietor, were once proprietors themselves, or are directly descended from such ex-proprietors. Their ancestors, or they themselves, failed to pay their revenue, the inexorable sale-law came into operation, and the proprietary interest passed away from men of blood and family to the man of money-bags. Thank Heaven! the evil days have gone by when such transfers of property, disinheriting hundreds at a blow, were common. But their mark remains behind like the trail of the serpent, full of venom and misfortune. Villages inhabited by large bodies of high-spirited men, such as the Brahmins or Rajpoots, whose rights in the land have been sold for revenue default, form the plague-spot in our administration. They are a continual thorn in the side of every revenue or police officer in their neighbourhood. The great object of the dispossessed clan is by continual worrying, by opposition both active and passive, by threats and violence, to bring the purchaser of their rights to terms, so as to leave them still virtually in their ancient position as proprietors. If this object be attained, well and good; if not, a perpetual civil war rages in the village. The nearest police station, and sooner or later, the magistrate's court, is filled with complaints of affray, assault, arson. Everybody in authority is against the ex-proprietors, from the magistrate down to the village-watchmen; but they are strong in numbers, and in the sympathies of their neighbours. If they torment the criminal authorities, they drive the revenue officers to despair;—summary suits for balances of rent, complaints of illegal attachment, exaction, and ouster, come in thick as hail; until everybody in the collector's court wishes that these unruly tenants were anywhere but in their district. The upshot of all this is, either that the purchaser gives up his bargain in despair, or that he buys over one part of the proprietary clan to his own interest, when the heads of the opposition party generally find their way into jail, and their descendants gradually subside into a reckless indigent peasantry. But, we repeat, thank Heaven, the causes which led to such evils have been removed. No man henceforth in the north-western provinces will fall from the rank of a proprietor to that of a tenant, except by his own fault, or by the operation of misfortunes which may overtake and subdue man under any system of government. The class of tenants just described should be treated by the ruling powers with firmness, yet with consideration, and should be encouraged to retrieve their fortunes by habits of industry. Holding, generally, large tracts of land, there is plenty of room for them to thrive if only they will learn to be thrifty; and the sooner they are taught that lawless habits end in ruin, and that to attain success in life they must deserve it, the better it will be for all parties. We may dismiss this unfortunate class of tenants with the remark, that their habits of life and domestic economy do not readily accommodate themselves to their fallen fortunes, and that, in consequence, they are almost always in debt and difficulties, and living on the verge of a predatory and lawless career.

Next to them come the large families of the same blood, who, from whatever cause, lost their proprietary rank and independence centuries ago. Such communities often live in contented subordination to their superior, paying perhaps a fixed rent for their estate, which they levy amongst themselves; and, on the whole, are not much worse off than the communities of cultivating proprietors.

After the Brahmin and Rajpoot cultivator in point of blood, but far superior to them in agricultural skill and industry, come the Jat and Kachi tribes. Then follow a variety of families, who are seldom found as proprietors, but who cultivate the soil in patches of varying extent in almost every village. Some of these nearly monopolise peculiar crops; as, for instance, the Kahar or bearer caste, who generally grow the singhara in pools, and hemp in light soils, as well as the ordinary cereals. Taking these cultivators in the mass, they are, as we might expect, a lower race, perhaps morally, and certainly physically, than the owners of the land. Centuries of subordination to village tyranny have left these men servile, timid, and deceitful. They are, however, more sinned against than sinning; humble, patient, and industrious, but withal slippery and cunning; living from hand to mouth; depending more or less on the favour of the village proprietor, and his creature, the village accountant; we must not expect to find amongst them the severer virtues of our race. It is no small credit to them to say, that though often driven to satisfy their hunger by parching the unripe crops in the corner of a field, yet they generally pay their rents honestly. Their houses surround the fort in which the heads of the village dwell, and stretch out to the edge of the cultivation. The coarsest bread, with the rare addition of a little sugar, or ghee, satisfies their hunger. A cloth round their loins made in the village loom, and a rough woollen blanket made by the village shepherd for winter, complete their ordinary dress. A few brass pots, rude ploughs and well-ropes, form their capital; a few toil-worn bullocks, with perhaps a milch cow or buffalo, form their live-stock. The early dawn sees thousands of these hard-working men plodding forth to their daily task in winter: the summer moon shines on their labours all night long. Like the patriarch of old, "in the day the drought consumes them, and the frost by night, and the sleep departs from their eyes."

Yet, thanks to the blessing of a *fixed rent*, these cultivators form on the whole a happy and contented race. The payments made by them, whether in money or kind, cannot be raised at the discretion of any one; nor, if their rent is paid, can they be removed from their land. However much this may limit the value of the superior proprietary right, no man who has observed the working classes in India can doubt the efficacy of a fixed moderate rent to promote the greatest happiness of the greatest number. It has been prettily written by some one, that " no man who owns a tree and loves it can be desolate." Words cannot describe the comfort and comparative independence which the holding and owning (by, however, a vile sort of ownership) a little plot of ground brings to millions of our Eastern subjects. All that volume of affection which the Englishman bestows upon his fireside, the Irishman on his pig and potato-ground, the Scotchman on his heather-clad mountains,—all that the Frenchman feels or professes to feel for Paris and "*la belle France*," or the American for the star-spangled banner,—in short, all the feelings which in other lands centre in family love or patriotic pride, are concentrated by the Indian peasant on his land. Beyond it, beyond the range of his own village and the nearest mart for village produce, he seldom bestows a thought. Little cares he who rules the land, so long as he is left in secure possession of his little speck of it. The fierce strife which so often scorches the souls of the land-owners, the vexatious lawsuits, the wearisome attendance in courts of law, —all this the tenant, under ordinary circumstances, escapes. If his life be one of toil and privation, it is sweetened by the love which he bears to his land —land which his father ploughed before him, and his sons should plough when he has passed away.

India is the land of contrasts. We know of none more striking than the contrast between agricultural appliances and agricultural results. An Englishman, fresh perhaps from the loams of Yorkshire or the clays of Essex, sees a miserable-looking peasant with a single cloth round his loins, creeping out late in June with what looks like a crooked stick on his shoulder, and urging before him a couple of bullocks, which for size and condition a donkey on Hampstead Heath might despise. The country around is like a desert of sand, the wind like the blast from a furnace. However, a shower of rain falls, the bullocks are hitched on to the crooked stick, and begin to scratch the sand in little unequal rings, not a bit like the honest ankle-deep furrows of England. But what is the result of this simple process, so little resembling the three-horse ploughing, patent scarifying, bone-dust and guano doctoring of our home soil? Why, in November, if our Englishman goes again to the scene of the operations which appeared to him so contemptible, he will find himself in a forest of vegetation, and unable to see his way amidst fields of *jowar* or *bajera*, each plant standing nine feet high, and each ear of the corn weighing half a pound avoirdupoise.

The grain, ground and made into coarse heavy cakes, supplies the food of the cultivator till the spring harvest furnishes him with wheat, pulse, and barley. It becomes us not to speak with disrespect of agriculturists who knew the use of the drill-plough, and understood well the rotation of crops, at a time when England was a wilderness. If the proceedings of the peasantry in India, especially for the crop which grows almost spontaneously amidst the heat and moisture of the rainy season, be rude and simple, they yet display both skill and perseverance in the harder labours which raise their early or spring crops. The industrial energies of the human race are, perhaps, in no part of the world more fully developed than in the villages of Jats or Kachis, whether proprietors or mere tenants. Go when you will amongst their rich and well-manured fields, you find men, women, and children at work. Lands prepared by them (we speak now particularly of the Kachi or other gardening tribes) will bear comparison with any that could be shown in the gardens at Chatsworth or Kew. Acres and acres of rich soil, naturally tenacious but improved by incessant tillage, are annually prepared for sugar-cane and poppy cultivation, every lump as big as a hazel-nut being pulverised by repeated ploughings, or by thumping with a short wooden club, if other means fail. No living being works harder than the Kachi. In October he sows wheat or barley; in March or April he harvests it, and puts in a crop of water-melons or gourds; these by constant irrigation will be ripe in June, when comes the autumnal crop of millet, &c. And here again we meet with a contrast: the finest, stoutest, and most powerful of the inhabitants produce the worst crops. This is easily accounted for by the pride of high caste, which withers whatsoever it touches. Some of the Brahmins and Rajpoots are too proud to handle a plough. The Brahmin is unwilling to destroy animal life with the ploughshare or in spreading out manure: above all, he fears lest with the goad he should shed the blood of the sacred ox. The Rajpoot avoids the plough for the same reasons, after he has assumed the *juneo* or sacred thread round his neck, and sometimes postpones or entirely avoids this investiture in consequence. But pride of caste, like other sorts of pride, is modified a good deal by circumstances; and this agricultural exclusiveness, which is observed strictly by the people of the rich Benares province, who can afford to be supercilious, is little regarded to the north of Allahabad, where from various causes the demand for labour is greater.

The prevailing modes of cultivation in the north-west provinces have been well described in a late pamphlet by Mr. Coverley Jackson.* We gather the following memoranda as to the average hire of labour and rent in Upper India from Mr.

* "Statistics of Agra, by C. C. Jackson, Esq., C. S., Collector and Magistrate. Agra, 1850." In which will be found not only much useful statistical and agricultural information, but also some very just remarks on the injury which our mode of civil procedure may entail upon the landed proprietors; of which subject more hereafter.

Jackson's Statistics, modified by our own observations elsewhere.

*Rent.**

Money rent varies from 15 rs. an acre to 1 r. 4 as. Average rents may be set down thus :—

Land of the 1st quality. The very best land, in which tobacco, poppy, caraway seeds, safflower, and garden stuffs are grown, lets at 3 rs. per village begah, or 15 rs. per acre.

Land of the 2d quality. From 12 rs. 8 as. per acre to 7 rs. 8 as. Crops as in first quality, or wheat.

Land of the 3d quality. From 5 rs. to 1–4 per acre. In this land all the more ordinary cereals, also sugar-cane, indigo, and cotton, are produced. Garden ground is seldom rented so low as this, except where there are no good masonry wells for irrigation. The proportion of each quality of land is about as follows :—

| | | | |
|---|---|---|---|
| 1st | Quality, | $2\frac{1}{2}$ | per cent. |
| 2d | „ | $6\frac{1}{2}$ | „ |
| 3d | „ | 91 | „ |

*Labour.*

*Ploughing* in light sandy soils may be done at the rate of about one-half acre per diem ; the hire of ploughman, plough, and a pair of small bullocks, being about four anas. A working day for one pair of bullocks is from sunrise to noon.

* We may remind the English reader that a rupee is worth about two shillings, and contains sixteen anas.

*Irrigation.*—One pair of bullocks in six hours, with three men, will irrigate one-fifth of an acre.*

*Weeding.*—In a country like India, where vegetation is so rapid, the weeds would destroy the autumnal crop but for constant weeding. Average hire of men, women, and boys, one with another, is little more than 1½ ana per diem.

*Reaping.*—The labourer gets one sheaf in twenty, and takes care to bind good heavy ones for his own use, which the owner winks at, unless he be more than usually churlish. But customs vary, the general rule being that the reaper gets 8 to 10 lbs. weight of ears of corn for his day's work.

Rent payable by the ryots or tenants to the superior landholders is either in money or kind. Payments in kind are becoming less common every year, and prevail most in the wilder parts of the country. In unhealthy rough parts (such as the belt of jungle under our mountain ranges, for instance) the tenant gets two-thirds, or even three-fourths, of the crop; in more favoured places his share is about one-half of the produce. The landlord's share is given to him as it stands, or divided at the granary, as may be most convenient; sometimes it is converted into money by appraisement. Like most purely agricultural folk, the ryot has an

* It is supposed that the water is thirty-six feet below the surface, and that one superficial inch of water is led over the land. The cost of the apparatus and labour of man and beast per diem will be about eight or ten anas.

eye for valuation, which, when there is nothing to give it a bias, is unerring; he can tell to a few pounds' weight the outturn of a crop of standing corn. One custom is curious and worthy of mention, as throwing light on the manners of the people. A proprietor who has a good opinion of his tenant's honesty will allow him to cut and store his grain without any restriction. When the harvest is over, the landlord takes as his share whatever the tenant gives him. This settlement, "*in foro conscientiæ*," is called *Ram Kotulea*, or God's store, *i. e.* a share given fairly as in the sight of God.

It will at once strike our readers that there are grave objections to a system of rent which discourages exertion; for few men work heartily to improve the land when another is to share immediately in the produce. The system of payments in kind leads also to tedious disputes. Its good point is, that in catchy, uncertain spots or seasons, the landlord and tenant take all risks together.* The ryots, such as we have attempted to describe them, form the bulk of the labouring agricultural population, and far exceed in number the men who are mere farm-servants, or what we should call *labourers* at home. Farm-servants are found generally in the employ of the higher proprietary classes. Ploughmen, mostly of the *chumar* or leather-working caste,

* The plan of taking rents in kind is sometimes called indifferently Kunkoot or Bhutai; but the meaning of these terms is, strictly speaking, different. Kunkoot means appraisement of produce; bhutai (from bhaut, division) means division of produce.

do all sorts of rough out-of-door work, and receive about two rupees monthly hire, and about ten pounds weight of grain for each plough at the time of the spring and autumnal harvests. If they are used also for domestic work in-doors, a small gratuity is given occasionally, and a suit of clothes at family weddings. The village potter, ironsmith, carpenter, barber, and washerman, get a large handful of ears of corn at the time of cutting the harvest, and about ten pounds weight of the grain for each plough in the village when housed.

Below these, again, there is a class of agricultural slaves.* We use the word *slaves* for these domestic servants, either descended from parents of their own class, or the children of poor people adopted by the wealthy; but they are in reality free to go where they please, and only stay with their master so long as it suits their own pleasure. In return for all sorts of domestic service they get food, clothes, and protection, marry amongst their own class, and are not much worse off than the rest of the labouring poor.

As a general rule, the lower castes are ready to do any service suited to their capacity which the village proprietor requires; they attend his wedding

* These are called *khana-zad*, born in the family; or *goolam*, slave; *sirkaree*, *i.e.* belonging to the head of the establishment; *chela* or *chera*, dependant; *roteya*, who get food in lieu of wages; *ruhcoa*, destitute persons taken to stay in a family (from *ruhna*, to remain). The females are called *loundie*, *bandhees*, *bundoor*, *dasee*, and *cheree*; concubines of this class are called *sureet*.

processions, run messages, and are ready to serve him on all occasions. Perhaps one of the most striking points of resemblance between eastern and western politics is the sort of serf-like feeling displayed by the lower agricultural tribes on the one hand, and the patronising care of them shown on the other by their feudal superior the zemindar. In well-ordered villages, where the natural manners of the people are still in full operation, there is a real feeling of identity of interest between the higher and lower classes, and they are ready to fight the battles, attest the falsehoods, and further the devices one of another.

Such, then, are the peasants of the East, or of that part of it which falls within the scope of our observations. Compared with the peasantry of Europe, their lot is fortunate enough, so far as material prosperity and physical comfort are concerned. If they suffer from a burning sun, they avoid the severer privations which are caused by the cold of northern countries. If their food be coarse and simple, so is their taste; if their clothing be scanty, it is yet sufficient. If a famine once or twice a century decimate the population, they avoid the continual dearth of Europe. If their houses be rude and ill furnished, they are at all events rent-free and roomy enough. The English labourer, poor fellow, whilst he sweats over another man's fields, is looking gloomily forward to the time when his strength will fail to keep him longer out of "the Union,"—the Indian labourer is happily free from such dismal forebodings. Go into his house, except just before the harvest season (when he is now and then on short commons) and you will see piles of large earthen jars full of grain, and very often a good cow or buffalo to give milk and ghee to the family.

Would that we could give as good an account of the *morale* of these people as we honestly can of their *physique*. They may, perhaps, be less dissolute on the whole, and less brutal than the looser part of the European poor, but we shall look in vain amongst them for the rugged honesty of the English labourer, the native polish of the French *paysan*, or the simplicity of the Italian *contadino*. Of the Indian peasantry we fear it must be said, emphatically, " the truth is not in them." A lie seems to come to their lips almost more naturally than the truth. This is much from an habitual and hereditary servile and timid spirit, ever taught to prefer the expedient to the right. But how can moral right be found in the mazes of a wrong religion? when the fountain head is corrupt, where shall we look for the clear stream of truth and virtue? 'Tis sad to know that so debased is the state of millions of men,—men patient, laborious, and frugal—fit for better things. Sadder still will it be, if we quietly acquiesce in the moral depravity around us. Be it far from us to fold the hands in patient indifference, to turn away our heads and hearts with scorn: such is never our duty as men, as Englishmen, as Christians. For what purpose has Providence brought us mysteriously, almost miraculously, to the height upon which we stand, if we dare not to look around us, to look forward and to see India awakening from the torpor of ages, flinging away her ancient superstitions, and accepting from her conquerors the blessings of truth? Every Englishman in India has his mission. True, we cannot all sow the good seed; our secular engagements, our public duties forbid it. But who or what shall hinder us from breaking (so far as God may help) the stubborn soil? When God said, "Let there be light," the glorious work was all His own; yet were there (may we believe) thousands of ministering spirits to roll away the bands of night. So when the blessed Light shall shine on India (and who can tell how soon the clouds may be dispersed?), how many labourers may be called to prepare her soil for the heavenly influence! There is work for every man and woman amongst us. Our actions, our motives, are scrutinised by thousands of observant and intelligent men. Who can say how the silent eloquence of a virtuous life shall speak to their souls? But it is not only by example and by influence, those grand levers of the human affections, that we may hope to move these heathen hearts,—we may do more than this, we may exert ourselves directly for the benefit of the people. To give one instance: the natives are ignorant; and it has been too much the fashion to despise their own existing educational resources, and to take for granted that nothing short of a miracle can elevate native morals and manners. Now, why should we not try to improve the native schools, and thus to give the popular mind a better direction? We cannot enter here on the vast question of national education, but may just remind our readers, that where there is a will to be useful a way will be found. The local Government has set us all the example, and, superior to the senseless prejudices of former days, has stooped to visit and to inspect the indigenous schools. Every one may, if he please, help on this good work. And if it be granted that knowledge is better than ignorance, science better than quackery, then surely it is a noble work to shape aright the rising mind of the country, to give a true direction thereto instead of a false direction, —bread instead of a stone. As we cannot dispense with the village schools, why not strive to improve those nurseries of the Hindoo soul? Why not put useful books instead of trash into the hands of the young? Once the taste for sound pabulum felt, the healthy appetite will grow with what it devours. Tales about fabulous gods, demons, and puppet-kings, will be thrown aside when the true lights of history and science dawn upon the mind. If any human means can, under the blessing of the Omnipotent, prepare His way, the means of education are not to be neglected. We cannot give all the instruction we would; our eyes, our son's eyes, may not see the light of God break forth upon India, but, we repeat it, this is no reason for refusing to dispel the darkness.

If we would discharge our duty to our neighbours and ourselves, we must be up and doing. To stand aloof, lest by meddling with heathen schools we defile ourselves, is not to follow the example of the great Missionary, who, going forth to instruct the heathen world, made himself "all things to all men, if by any means he might save some."

# V.

## DOMESTIC HISTORY OF THE RAJPOOT FAMILY.

---

The name of Lord William Bentinck is, in the north-western provinces of India, usually associated with the idea of progress and reform. His temperament qualified him for the task of flinging down, with a strong hand, every apparent obstacle to improvement, and his career was essentially an onward career. But, when the occasion demanded it, he could retrace with cautious steps the ground which his predecessors had too rashly occupied. Great as a reformer, he was greater still as a conservative. We might prove this assertion by other instances, but it will satisfy our present purpose to give one example of this wise *retrograde* policy.

From the days of Timour downwards, every great statesman in India had been, to use Timour's own words, "the Lord of the Sword and the Pen."* To separate the department of justice from the department of revenue, the sword of the magistrate from the cutcherry of the revenue

* "Institutes of Timour," book ii.

officer, had formed no part of the policy of any chief until Lord Cornwallis and the Code of 1793 came to sweep away the Indian, and to introduce the English régime. Ten or twelve years after this epoch, the new system had worked its way to Madras, and it was there that its absurdity was most thoroughly exposed by Colonel Munro. He himself was equally able to wield the sword of the conqueror or the pen of the statesman, and versed as he was in every detail of revenue management, no man was better qualified to lift the veil of adulation and pretension which had so long been thrown over the Cornwallis legislation.* No man better than Munro could point at once to the mistakes and injustice of that feeble, though well-meant policy, and never did the arguments of Munro tell more strongly, than when he showed the impolicy of separating the revenue from the police power. From Sir Thomas Munro, Lord W. Bentinck took many a valuable lesson, and before introducing his great revenue reforms throughout Upper India, his Lordship wisely and boldly united the offices of magistrate and collector.† This was a step, if we are to believe the political economists of Europe, *backwards*, but in reality a wise and humane one.

The separation of the revenue *bureau* from the

* "A monument of human wisdom." This was the term applied to the Code of 1793, by one of its supporters.

† It is true that such union had been *legalized* in 1821, but it was not carried into execution till ten years after by Lord W. Bentinck.

court of the magistrate, which the jealousy of the middle classes, and perhaps the progress of civilisation, has enforced in Europe, is not suited to the existing state of things, or, rather, to the state of the national mind, in the East. Before we came here, the head of every village, of every province, of each state, had a mixed revenue and judicial power. This is what the people are used to; they are prepared to respect a chief, who, if he takes their revenue with one hand, administers speedy and substantial justice with the other.

But they could never understand the theory of an office which gave a man the power to seize and sell a whole province for revenue default, whilst he could not arbitrate between a landlord and tenant in the most trivial matter. They will never respect an official who can only take their money, and beyond that has no power either to protect or to punish them; but to a chief who holds the sword of the magistrate as well as the pen of the tax-gatherer they will pay all honour and respect. The officer of Government feels this; he knows that the people almost worship him; and, if he is worth his salt, he strives to feel for them and with them. No longer tempted, as a mere collector of revenue, to consider all men as revenue-payers only, no longer provoked as a magistrate to conclude, as some magistrates have done, that all men are rogues, his position is exalted as much as his power is increased. The collector's influence is extended, but so, too, is the interest which he feels for the people. The authority of the magistrate is advanced, but so in proportion is the temper of his administration softened and improved. Increased power is attended with wider sympathies and a deeper sense of responsibility.

All this, we know, has been disputed, but we have neither time nor inclination to raise the ghosts of all the objections which were decently interred by Munro so long back as 1815. Nobody at the present time, that we know of, denies in this particular instance the advantages resulting from our return to the old policy of the country.

The experience of every day teaches us more and more that the true course of the Indian legislator must consist in the moulding, the suiting, and if need be, the *lowering** his proceedings so as to meet the mind of the people. If it be good for India to climb the heights of European political science, the ascent will never be made unless we first step down into their own *arena* to lend them a helping hand. Our desire in these "Notes" is to describe to our readers the country people as they are, and as they are affected by the policy of our Government, and we wish, on the present occasion, to show the advantages resulting from the *combined* action of the magistrate and collector.

With this object before us, we shall make no apology for the insertion of the following simple narration, taken from the "*note-book*" of a friend, who, as magistrate and collector of a district, has

* Of course we do not speak of lowering our policy *morally*, but *artistically*; in other words, simplifying, and, as it were, diluting it, to suit the taste of the people.

had opportunities of watching the effect of our institutions upon the mind of the people. We give prominence to the extract the more readily because we believe that simple details of official life in India, which, from some cause or other, are seldom given to the public, may be useful, and not without interest to our readers. This tale seems to us to show forcibly how well the collector may aid the magistrate under the existing system.

*Camp, Dec.* 18.—Before I forget a day's work I lately had, let me try to make some note of it. To begin at the beginning. It was, I well remember, a burning day last July, when Kumaloodeen, my deputy-collector, first came to me about the Mullowlie case. The rain kept off, and the sky was clouded with dust, which obscured the sun like the ashes from a volcano. We used just then to have cutcherry open from before six in the morning till eleven, but even at that early hour the poorer of the omlah, and suitors who had to walk home, were occasionally struck down by *coup de soleil* on their way. I had left the court, and was sitting down to my mid-day breakfast, when the deputy was announced. I felt disinclined at the moment to receive a visitor, but, knowing that he was a man of business, who would not come a mile out of his way (when the thermometer was standing at 120°) without some good reason, I ordered him to be shown in at once. Kumaloodeen is a fine-looking man, like most Rohilla gentlemen, stout, and broad made, with a clear, calm eye, aquiline nose, and pleasing *contour* of face. He had worked his way up from the place of an ordinary scribe to be serishtadar, or head man of the Revenue Court in the district; and when the orders for creating deputy-collectors came out, he was one of the first natives raised to that honourable office. He proved himself well deserving of the promotion; just, experienced, and of good ability, he was beloved and respected by the native population, who looked upon him as a father and a friend. The pergunneh of M——, which, since the time of the famine, had been out of order, was under his charge, and a revision of the settlement having been made, that part of the country was beginning to prosper again about the time my story begins. After the usual salutations,—

*Deputy.*—"I have come to speak to you, Sir, about the Mullowlie estate. You remember Mullowlie—it is old Holasi's village, in which you ordered me to make a partition of the land. Well, I have completed the matter so far as the land is concerned, but the family cannot agree amongst themselves about the division of their dwelling-house." (*Here Kumaloodeen dropped his voice, and glanced around,—I ordered the servants to leave the room,—when he proceeded*)— "In the house treasure is secreted to a large amount, nobody knows *where*, except the old man, Holasi; but all the family know that money is buried *somewhere.* Now, Sir, what I am afraid of is, that as the old man and his nephew have quarrelled about their land, they will go on disputing about the house and the treasure ; an attempt will be made to dig for the coin, when there will be a fight, and some of the Thakoors will be killed, or, what is almost as bad, they will commence proceedings the one against the other in the civil courts. In either case the family will be ruined, and that will be a pity, as they are as fine a set as any in the pergunneh."

*Collector* (*smiling*).—"I wonder, Mr. Deputy, if Providence had made you a '*Moonsiff*,' instead of a '*Deputy-Collector*,' whether you would have been more lenient in your strictures upon our system of civil justice?"

*Deputy*.—"Ask our Sudder Ameen, Sir, who is a zemindar himself, as well as a civil judge, whether any family of landholders, who once get a taste for going to law, ever stop whilst a pice is left them? Heaven protect us from civil law, a taste for it is just like a taste for opium-eating, or gambling. But, Sir, excuse me, I was going to say that the Mullowlie people have all solemnly promised me to put off further dispute, and all division of their property, such as houses, grain, stacks, &c., till the cold weather: *then* I want you to go the village for a few hours, when you can have the money dug up and divided, and I know you will be glad to save the family from either broils or litigation."

*Collector*.—"If the people apply to me I shall be glad to do what I can to settle their disputes ;

in the meantime, the less said about this treasure the better. But how much is there?"

*Deputy.*—"From ten to twenty thousand rupees, if report is to be trusted."

I had forgotten all about this conversation when lately I came to spend a few days in the M—— pergunneh. Kumalooden came out there to meet me, and our camp was pitched, as it happened, within seven or eight miles of Mullowlie.

I had made my usual march one morning, and was hearing my police reports after breakfast; old Sheikh Kulloo was opening them in a corner of my tent, and reading, spectacle on nose, in the regular orthodox sing-song tone, interlarding his recitative with an occasional remark, generally complimentary to me, or the reverse of complimentary to any police official who might not happen to be in his good books.

*Sheikh Kulloo, loquitur (very rapidly, and in the Oordoo - Persic jargon of the Foujdarree courts.)* "No event of any importance noted "from thanah Junglepoor — two old women "tumbled into wells—one man gored by a bul-"lock—one attempt at burglary—one little boy "lost at the Dèvee mèlah—one burkundaz wants "leave of absence;"—(sing-song ends—the Sheikh speaks in his blandest natural tones,)—"The pros-"perity of your honour is so great, that to open "these daily thanah reports is now almost super-"fluous. I remember the time when we used to "have gang-robberies every month; and highway "robberies, attended with wounding, every fort-"night: but now, owing to the great good fortune" .... here the Naib Nazir was interrupted by the entrance of a very important personage (in his own opinion), Rung Lal, acting tehsildar of M——, who stated that he had just received an express from the neighbouring police-officer of Junglepoor, to the effect that a robbery of four thousand rupees had taken place at Mullowlie. Rung Lal expressed his desire to go at once to the spot, and to assist in the investigation. "Four thousand rupees!" said I: "impossible; I don't believe it." "Four thousand rupees!" groaned Sheikh Kulloo; "this is the end of the year, and "here comes a case of four thousand rupees— "the criminal statements are utterly spoilt. Well, "there is no struggling against destiny; what is "to be, surely comes to pass; but, Sir, your "slave always told you that the thanadar of Jun-"glepoor was a *kum-bukt*,—a man born under "an evil omen; and you, with your usual saga-"city...." "Now, Sheikh," I interrupted, "put "up your papers, reach me my spurs, and go over "to give my compliments to the Deputy Sahib; "he must go with me." In five minutes we were on our horses, and proceeding at a hand-gallop towards Mullowlie. *En route*, let me describe my companion, the tehsildar Rung Lal. This man had been for thirty years in Government employ in the district, and for the last ten as serishtadar of the collector's office. Formerly he used to take bribes, and to intrigue as much as other Kayeths generally do, but of late years (possibly with an eye to official promotion) he had been very guarded and correct in his conduct. He was a large, heavy-looking man, of great capacity for business, and much experience. But, his late promotion to the office of tehsildar had turned his head a little; and as we rode along he delivered himself of a constant stream of self-gratulation.

*Rung Lal.*—" It was high time for you to send me out to M——; what do you think I found there at the tahseely?—seven burkundaz; yes, Sir, *seven*, too old to walk, and riding about on ponies to collect the revenue; no regular office hours, and two hundred and seventeen bats; yes, live bats in the Government Treasury! Then, Sir, there were . . . ." (here Rung Lal stopped short, observing, perhaps, a cloud on my brow, and almost a tear in the eye of his predecessor, a fine old man, who having grown grey in the service, and expecting a pension, was on a smart pony close behind us, listening to our conversation.

*Collector.*—" Well, Rung Lal, we will talk about that another day. You have had a good harvest, and the spring-crops look well."

*Rung Lal.*—" By your good fortune, Sir, since I came here there has been a wonderful crop; and as for the revenue, which used always to be behind, it is paid up to the day."

*Collector.*—" Good; how do you like the people? I hope you get on well with them?"

*Rung Lal.*—"Well with them! Indeed I do;

they are *shureer* (rebellious), very *shureer*, but they are afraid of me; besides which, I put them to no expense; when I go to the villages I won't even take a drink of water from them; in short, I . . ."

*Collector* (*getting tired of Rung Lal and his puffs*).—" What is the name of this village?"

*Rung Lal.*—" Mobarikpoor. I have been in this pergunneh four months and ten days only, but I know the name of every village in it. Mobarikpoor is a famous place for tobacco."

*Collector.*—" What are those blackened earthen pots stuck upon sticks in the tobacco? They look like scare-crows, but surely neither bird nor beast will touch the tobacco."

*Rung Lal* (*with a subdued chuckle*).—" No, Sir, those are not scare-crows, but charms. The crop, you see, is good, and those pots are put up to catch the envious (or evil) eye of the passer-by; by the goodness of Providence I am versed in all rural customs, though I have lived so many years in a city."

Just here we met the owners of the village, who, on hearing that a *hākim* was passing by, had hurried out to make their salaams. " What," cries Rung Lal, " come out without your turban to see the Collector! For shame!"

*Collector.*—" Never mind." (To the zemindars, who were looking rather abashed), " Well, my men, you have some nice land here, and a fine village. Have you a school for your sons?"

*Zemindars.*—" We are poor men, my Lord;

are we to eat or to send our boys to school? The tehsildar Sahib knows . . . ."

*Rung Lal.*—"I know you to be a pack of ill-fated asses. Although I attend punctually to every part of the duties of the 'Companee Buhadoor,' if there is one thing I pay more attention to than another, it is the promotion of education. But these men, and such as these who prefer food to knowledge, oppose me. However, I could get on well enough but for the old women and the putwarries, who are always putting some new idea into people's heads. When I first came here, nothing would please them but that the Government would make *Feringees* of all the little boys. When the people gave up this notion a new fancy was brought out: sixteen schools out of four-and-twenty in the jurisdiction of your humble servant were stopped; yes, absolutely closed; and what, Sir, do you suppose was the reason? The old women spread a report that the Ganges canal, which has been so long cutting, would not *chul*, that the water would not run in it, and that the boys were not really wanted for *education*, but for *sacrifice* to propitiate Gunga-jee! The schools, as I say, were deserted until I went round to the villages, and swore upon the Ganges water that there was no real cause for alarm."

But enough of Rung Lal and his prosing—to do him justice, he has made a very good tehsildar so far, and will do well, I doubt not.

It was noontide when we rode into Mullowlie.

At the entrace of the village, a well-dressed young man, with a very dejected look, met us, and made a salaam. Supposing him, rightly, to be one of the zemindars of the place, I inquired whether any theft had taken place, to the amount of four thousand rupees. He said, "Yes, Sir, and *I* am the thief." "That is just what I told you, Sir," said the deputy; "the family feuds are breaking out "again, and you have come in time to settle them. "Depend on it, no theft has happened at all." By this time we had reached the fort, in which the Thakoor chiefs lived. Riding under the spacious doorway into the outer court, which surrounded the house, I observed an old man sitting, sunning himself on a sort of bench, who made a salaam to me, and called out that he had lost the use of his legs, or he would have got up to welcome me. This was Holasi, the head of the family, whose tale I may here tell as shortly as I can. Holasi is a Chowhan Thakoor, the elder of two brothers, who, unlike the generality of their tribe, were celebrated twenty years ago for their economy, prudence, and untiring industry. They had amassed a considerable sum of money, and owned the large Mullowlie estate, as well as other distant villages. The fame of their wealth having got abroad, a party of dacoits determined to attack Mullowlie. In the dead of the night Holasi was roused up, found his brother engaged hand-to-hand with the robbers, and arrived, with others of the family, only in time to save the life of his infant nephews, and to avenge the death of his brother, who fell covered with wounds. Holasi took paternal charge of his nephews, and a little niece, who, with the widow of his brother, lived with his own family in the Mullowlie fort. Some eight years after this domestic tragedy, the settlement of the land revenue of Mullowlie came on, and Holasi very honestly entered in the village papers the names of his nephews as joint-proprietors with himself in the Mullowlie estate. No Rajpootnee damsel in the district had a better dower or a gayer wedding than Holasi's niece. The nephews were brought up with their cousin Bijayee Singh, the only son of Holasi. In due time the elder nephew, Ewuz Singh, who, notwithstanding his uncle's kindness to him, was of a jealous, suspicious temper, was married to the daughter of a Khuteyar Thakoor, and from that time there was an end to peace and harmony in the Mullowlie family. As soon as Ewuz was settled with his wife, and with every comfort around him which a Rajpoot could desire, he found out that he was an ill-used man. Forgetful of the many benefits he had received from his uncle, he determined upon a step which was most distasteful to the old chief. This was to sue in the collector's court for a separation of the landed estate, so that he might take the management of his ancestral share of the land out of Holasi's hands and into his own. Ewuz Singh was put up to this course by his wife's family, who wished to get the Mullowlie estate into their own clutches, if possible. They were encouraged to this the more that old Holasi had lately had an attack of palsy, and (as natives often do when they become infirm) had made over his own right and interest in his landed estates to his son, Bijayee Singh, who, being an easy open-hearted man, was supposed not to inherit his father's talent for business.

You might go a long way without finding a finer fellow than this Bijayee Singh. With a noble manly look, with all the innate courage and spirit of the Rajpoot, he was yet as gentle as a lamb. There was not a better shot, a more dashing rider, nor a more dexterous swordsman in the country side, yet he nursed and watched over his old father with the devotion of a woman. I have above hinted, that old Holasi was hurt when his nephew, Ewuz Singh, demanded his own share of the estate, and refused any longer to be satisfied with the abundant provision which he had hitherto enjoyed in common with the rest of the family. Now, it may seem very natural to the English mind, and very right for Ewuz Singh thus to insist upon his claiming his separate share, and *setting up*, as we call it, for himself; but, knowing how much happier the native families are living in patriarchal form together, I was very sorry when he came to the collector's court to claim his separate rights. Still I could offer no opposition to his demand for a division of the land according to the terms of the village settlement.

Old Holasi opposed him, disputed my authority to divide the land, and when other means failed appealed to the Commissioner, declaring that his nephew was under age, and not entitled to any division. The *Junm-puttr** was produced, and, like the parish register, there was no appealing from its testimony; so the division, or *butwarra*, as it is called in official parlance, proceeded under the superintendence of the native deputy-collector. Eventually, equal lots being made, the land measured, and mapped, the Mullowlie estate was divided. One *turuf* or side was given to Bijayee Singh, as the representative of Holasi, and the other to Ewuz Singh and his brother. The deputy has often told me, that during this transaction the only one of the parties who behaved with uniform temper and honest purpose was Bijayee Singh. True, under the influence of his father's authority he at first opposed the division, but when he saw that Ewuz Singh had the law clearly on his side, he put no further impediment in the way, and behaved fairly and honorably.

This, then, was the trio that assembled round me with their numerous followers, as I got off my horse and sat down in the shade of the porch. In this very spot, twenty years ago, Holasi had driven off the dacoits from the dead body of his brother. There he was now, almost unable to move, carried about by two men, or propped up in a corner with pillows, helpless in body, yet full of spirit and indignation. "Look, sir," he said, pointing to Ewuz, who stood with his head down in silent dejection, "look at that boy, who has brought ruin "upon Holasi's house. Ask him, who saved him

* This is a paper drawn out by the family Brahmin, showing the moment at which a child is born.

"from the dacoits? Who nursed and fed him? "Ask him whether in this pergunneh any Raj-"poot's daughter had such a wedding as his sister? "Ask him who gave her dower, yes, from an "elephant downwards,—who furnished her with "such jewels as Agra alone can supply?" "Stop, "father," said Ewuz, "*kusoor hooa*, I have erred; "now be pleased to ask the *hākim* to punish "me. I have ill-treated you, I have robbed you." "Come," said I, "let us hear the thanadar. I can "believe that Ewuz Singh has given you pain and "annoyance, old man; but can the son of a Cho-"han Thakoor rob his own relations?" Hereupon Bijayee Singh stepped forward—"Sir," said he, "yesterday I quarrelled with Ewuz Singh; in my "rage I went to the thana and accused him of "theft. I lied, Ewuz is no thief: we have a dis-"pute about our dwelling, but we are not thieves. "I am the one to blame; punish me."

I called up the thanadar, got pen and paper, held a short proceeding after taking one or two depositions, and inflicted a small fine on Bijayee Singh for having given false information to the police, advising him to keep his temper better in future. I then asked to be shown the disputed abode. Leaving the old man under the porch, we walked on. I never go over one of these fine old Rajpoot forts, without half envying the occupiers the quiet country life they lead:—there is such a rude abundance of farm produce, such sleek cattle and horses, such quiet shady spots and corners. Mullowlie was as nice a place of the sort as I had ever seen. Passing through a large open court, surrounded with roomy well-built stables and store-rooms, we came to a square two-storied house. I observed the deputy send on a man to order the females out of the way. The dwelling-house was built with blind high walls outside, but opening within into a quadrangular court, which was overlooked by the flat-terraced roofs and open verandahs, from which the women saw their little share of the world. The walls, where not painted with grotesque figures, sparkled with the fine white silver sand of the Doab, which was carefully plastered over them; implements for spinning, cleaning grain, and cooking, were strewed about; everything looked comfortable and home-like. The fact was, as I afterwards heard, the good folk of Mullowlie had quarrelled so violently amongst themselves the day before my visit, that no dinner had been cooked nor eaten. To make up for lost time, on the morning when I peeped into their house, an abundant meal was preparing; though, as we shall see presently, a second fast-day was in store for the family party.

Looking round at the rooms, terraces, galleries, verandahs, and endless mud walls, I thought to myself what a hopeless search the family might have for old Holasi's rupees if he died without disclosing their secret hiding-place. I was willing to test the truth of the story about this treasure; so, turning to the young men, I said, "Why do you "not divide your property? thus, one party take "this dwelling-house, which is highly finished "and very snug, no doubt, but somewhat confined, "and the other party take that fine range of houses "outside, with the large court attached?" They shook their heads, and I saw that the small dwelling-house, in which both had rooms at present, was the object of their desire.

I did not choose to allude to the treasure unless they mentioned it to me, and we returned to the outer gateway, where old Holasi was seated. After some conversation with the young men and the thanadar it was settled, that the division of the disputed dwellings should be decided by a *punchayet*, or jury composed of three neighbouring landholders, whose arbitration was agreed to by both the son and nephew of the old man. But he himself was not satisfied with this arrangement, and just as I was getting on my horse to return to my camp, I heard his voice. "Sir, sir, you must "stop; I want to speak to you." When I came up to him he seized me by the legs, and pressing his old head as well as he could towards my feet, he said, addressing me by my name, "You must not "go yet; you must do Holasi justice, or these lads "will fight and destroy themselves and me also. "There is *treasure* buried in Mullowlie fort, and "you must come and dig it up: I will show it to "nobody living, save in your presence or the deputy's. Lift me up, quick, my lads, and carry "me to the inner house."

Once again the women were scared away from their pursuits, as old Holasi, carried by his son and another stout fellow, pushed into the quadrangle. "Let me down *there*," screamed Holasi; "*there*."

The old man took his post in a room on the left side as we came in, where Ewuz Singh's wife had a moment before been cooking her husband's ample meal. Fires were blazing, and large vessels sending forth a savoury steam. "Away with all that; "out with the fire, scrape away the ashes," said Holasi: "and now, my boys, dig." Ewuz Singh said, "Sir, this is my house; you may dig here, but "you will allow me afterwards to dig in Bijayee "Singh's house opposite: *there* is the treasure, not "*here*." To this stipulation all assented. "The "money is in a *khulsa*" (large brass vessel), said Holasi, "and there are Rs. 10,000, more or less." Two sturdy dependants of Holasi's were soon working away, with that peculiar zeal which animates a native when he is digging down his neighbour's wall, whilst at every stroke of the spade Ewuz seemed to flinch as if it hurt him. The digging went on fast and furious, until at last the heads only of the diggers were visible. The natives with me began to exchange looks, and to hint to one another their doubts; my patience, too, was fast oozing away, when suddenly a spade struck upon an earthen pot, which breaking to shivers, left a heap of coin mixed with the earth. The rupees were soon handed up, cleaned and counted. They were old Furuckabad rupees, and numbered Rs. 2318.

"There are more," cried Holasi; "search for "the *khulsa*: you may blow me out of a gun if it is "not close at hand." After some half hour of hard work the spade of one of the diggers struck against a metal vessel, and the "*khulsa*" was found. "Pull "it out," cried I. "I can't," said the voice below, "it is brimful of rupees; and so heavy, it cannot "be moved." A rope was thrown over a beam in the roof, then let down into the pit where the diggers were, and fastened to the neck of the *khulsa.* A strong pull, off flew the head of the vessel, and down went the pullers into the dust. In due time the coin was picked out, and we all set to work, some washing, some counting, the village bunyan weighing, and two tailors in a corner stitching large double bags of cotton cloth, each big enough to hold two thousand rupees. The contents of the brass vessel turned out to amount to Rs. 6392, fine old Furuckabad rupees, which are now at a premium in the market owing to the purity of the silver.

Ewuz Singh now urged me to push the search further into the private rooms of his cousin Bijayee, on the opposite side of the quadrangle, assuring me that he could point out treasure there. The rooms were long and dark; a torch was sent for, but, from the rambling manner of Ewuz, I could see that he did not know where to look. At last he came to a place where the earth had newly been turned up. "Look, sir," he cried; "the villains, they have carried away the money." At last, getting desperate, he said, "I'll go and bring the old woman, my mother; she knows all about it." Away he rushed, and returned presently, supporting what looked like a bundle of clothes in his arms. The old lady, emerging from the folds, looked around, seemingly in a doting, scared manner, and then suddenly stretched out her arm, and, with a withered fore finger pointed to a distant wall. She was carried to the spot, and the digging commenced. About a foot below the surface Ewuz hit upon an earthen vessel. "Here, here are the rupees which my mother buried!" he cried with delight. "Stop," said I: "when did your mother bury her treasure?" "Twenty years ago." "Then this is not hers; for see, here is the head of Queen Victoria—whom may Heaven long preserve." In short, the rupees were some 1811 in number, which Bijayee Singh had buried at the end of the last harvest. Instead of putting his savings in an old stocking, as an English countryman might have done, or into a hole in the thatch like an Irishman,* he had, in the Indian fashion, buried them in the earth. All eyes were now turned upon the old woman, and surmises passed round as to the manner in which she, bed-ridden in a remote part of the house, had become acquainted with Bijayee Singh's treasure.

There she sat, with her shrivelled arm and

* Many of our readers may remember the story of the merchant at Delhi. On his father's death, this man was looking over the family account-books, when he found this entry:—

"When six *ghurrees* of the day were remaining on the first day of the month Phagoon, I buried one lac of gold mohurs in the dome of the Jumma Musjid."

The merchant, sorely puzzled, consulted the family physician, who, on being promised a share of the treasure, undertook to point it out. On the month and hour indicated he searched for the exact spot in the merchant's premises where the shadow of the dome fell, and there, sure enough, was the money.

skinny finger still pointing to the ground. Ewuz Singh went again to work, with two or three helpers. I came out into the court, and was turning over in my mind how I should best dispose of the money until the jury could be summoned to apportion it amongst the claimants, when a shout from within announced further discoveries. Ewuz Singh was up to his knees in rupees; he had come upon a large earthen *mone*, or urn, out of which we, in due time, counted and weighed 11,283 rupees. They were the same old-fashioned coinage as those which had come out of the *khulsa*. We had now altogether 21,804 rupees, which were being washed, piled, and weighed. I sat watching the work whilst the deputy went out, as he said, to say his afternoon prayers, taking old Holasi with him. To tell the truth, I felt a little perplexed. Evening was coming on; it was a wild corner of my district; what was I to do with all this money? The *punchayet* of neighbours were the best people to divide it, no doubt; but it was too late to send for them at that hour. Should I seal up the coin and send it to the tehsildar's cutcherry, until the arbitrators came to divide it, or —— ? Here the deputy came in and addressed me in an under-tone. "I have been "talking," said he, "to the old man, who will not "make any opposition if you propose to divide the "money at once, and to make over to each party "what came out of their own house." I asked whether Bijayee Singh would agree. The deputy answered—"Bijayee Singh cares nothing about "the money, but I have had much trouble in "persuading old Holasi, who says that all belongs "to him, though he did not deny that his brother "had been privy to its concealment." The sun had just gone down below the walls of the old fort, and there was little time for debate.

I addressed the cousins, reminding them that my only object was their common good, and asking them whether they chose to abide by my decision. They both assented eagerly. I turned to Ewus Singh and said, "I propose to give you all the "money that came out of your kitchen, being "rupees 8710; but," I added, "you must both "*agree* or I'll do nothing—say, are you satisfied?" "Yes, I am content." "Write it down," said I, "and sign your approval. In such a case I will "use no authority of my own; all I wish is to "see you both satisfied and reconciled."

All eyes were now turned on Bijayee Singh. The scene was a curious one. The women, unable to restrain their curiosity, had crept on to the roof close above us, forming, with their crimson veils and deep blue dresses, a picturesque group. Bags of money were piled around the court amidst a medley of pots, pans, wooden bowls, spades and pickaxes; in one corner two cats, who had contrived to upset a vessel of milk, were helping themselves, watching as intently their flowing treasure as their biped neighbours were eyeing the silver heaps. A group of stout Rajpoots pressed round Bijayee Singh, whilst apart from them stood the deputy, in his riding-boots, green cloth mantle, and handsome belt, in a careless attitude, but fully awake to all around him. On the opposite side sat I, pen in hand, noting down Ewuz Singh's agreement to the terms proposed. The friends of Bijayee Singh began to urge him not to give his money or his father's to the intruder who had brought discord into the family. He had stooped down over the coin, which had been brought out of his house, and lay there in a monstrous pile, enough to tempt the virtue of most men. Every breath was hushed as I asked again, in a loud voice, whether Bijayee Singh agreed to the terms proposed? The pen was waiting to take down his words, and it was just the moment when a man might be expected to make the best terms for himself. Bijayee Singh covered his face with his hands, and for a moment seemed in doubt; then, pushing far from him the silver pile, he said, "Take the money, sir, I have plenty; take "it all, give it to Ewuz; only ask him"—and here a tear trickled down his manly face—"ask him "to love Holasi and me, and not to bring dis-"sension into our home: other money I can get, "but where shall I find another brother?"*

Ewuz melted and fell at his cousin's feet. They embraced, and their voices trembled as they vowed to forget their strife, and to smooth with filial kindness the declining years of old Holasi. I felt proud of my Rajpoot friends. "Come, "come," I said, "let us not forget the feelings

* *Bhai* was the word used, which means brother or cousin.

"of this moment. Imitate the example of your "fathers—stick to one another, for better or for "worse, in life or in death, as they did; money "you may get, or land, but Bijayee Singh has "well said, Where can you find another brother?"

It was late; taking up, as a trophy, my share of the plunder, the rim which we had pulled off the brass pot, I told the thanadar and his attendant *burkundaz* to leave the fort. They obeyed, the latter taking off his shoes and shaking them, to show that none of the rupees had found their way in. Next went the tailors; when a gratuity was wanted for them, a member of the family tossed them one of the rupees from the treasure-heap. This was observed by the others, who forthwith took back the coin and gave a common rupee from their purse instead.

The deputy smiled and shook his head; "Ah," said he, "they will never touch these "rupees unless it be to save their land or to buy "more."

The moon shone as we trotted home to our camp, and that night I dreamed of Bijayee Singh and his rupees.*

* We have learned that the two cousins and the old man are living now on good terms, and talking of investing their spare cash in Company's paper. A further amicable division of the property has been made, the upshot of which was, that all grain, live-stock, arms, and utensils, were equally divided between the cousins, whilst for the head of the family the following articles were reserved:—

A tent, a wedding palkee, five carpets, one shawl, and a pair of camel-drums.

## VI.

### NOTES ON THE POLICE.

---

TWENTY years ago a circular letter was sent to the magistrates of the Bengal Presidency, requesting them *not to hamstring* convicts before execution!* Within the last few months the Government of the north-west provinces directed magistrates to exempt from the ordinary prison-rules of clipping and shaving, not only the sacred locks of Sikh prisoners, but the hair of all convicts to whom such a proceeding would be "justly offensive or degrading."† Straws thrown up show which way the wind blows, and, as the animus of the order of 1830 and the order of 1851 is equally benevolent, we can only conclude that the humanity of the present day takes a wider range, and pushes its sympathies farther than did the humanity of the last generation. If convicts

* Circular from Nizamut Adawlut to Magistrates, dated April 23, 1830.

† Letter from Secretary to Government, North-west Provinces, to Inspector of Prisons. 17th January, 1851.

were formerly treated like wild beasts, they are now treated like gentlemen, when they deserve it.

It may not be uninteresting to inquire whether any corresponding advance is to be observed in other branches of our penal law, and whether the people of the upper provinces have, on the whole, reason to be satisfied with the existing criminal code, and the manner of its administration. We have already attempted* to give our readers some account of the revenue system introduced into these provinces by our countrymen, and its bearing on the happiness of the people; it remains for us now to notice the effect on the same people of our proceedings as magistrates and conservators of the public peace.

It is an old saying, "when things come to the worst they must mend;" and we need not claim any great credit for English magistrates in Upper India, because the peace is better kept now than it was in the last century. They appeared upon the scene, at a time of anarchy, in a country never remarkable for order. But if we are to form any just conception of what the English have done for North-western India, we must take into full account the difficulties which beset their earliest steps as magistrates, as guardians of order and liberty. To say that they had to deal with a disordered or disorganised state of society would be scarcely enough; disorder or disorganisation implies previous order and organisation, but, at

* Notes on the Landed Tenures, p. 41.

the crisis of which we are writing, we may look in vain for any trace of either one or the other. No sooner did the hands of the Mahometan emperors slacken—and they had done so long before English cannons were heard in the Doab—no sooner had the scramble begun for the power of the old Mogul tyrants, than lawlessness became the law, misrule became the rule of the empire. In better days, some of the emperors, men of talent and power, had been able, with the help of their rough northern soldiers, to keep their dominions in subjection, and even to introduce some sort of public police for a short time, and within a narrow boundary. But civil order and liberty, if they ever existed, formed the exception, not the rule of the times. Eastern poets and historians love to dwell upon the virtues of kings, who left the delights of the seraglio to patrol their cities in the garb of a Kotwal, or who watched so closely over the public morals, that a purse of gold might be left with security on the highway. All this suits the Arabian Nights or the Mahometan historians of India equally well; but, as Mill says, we now know what value to put upon such statements. Shah Jehan had as many compliments paid to his police administration, and deserved them, as well as any of his predecessors, yet it was from his court that the travelling physician Bernier wrote so feelingly of "le peu d'argent qui me restoit de diverses rencontres de voleurs."

From the days of Shah Jehan down to the time when Lord Lake wrested Upper India from the grasp of the Mahrattas, there was no stronger government than that which Scindia created in the name and on the ruins of the Mogul empire. Particularly in the provinces assigned to his able general, Du Boigne, some degree of quiet was established, and the people were, to a certain extent, protected. But even there we may look in vain for anything like social order and civil liberty. In proportion as the head of the State was strong the people were weak. Ask any old man what was the condition of the Doab under the Mahrattas, and he will answer almost in the words of the Prophetess of Mount Ephraim,* "The highways "were unoccupied, and the travellers walked "through byways. The inhabitants of the vil-"lages ceased."

But already the leaven had been infused into the fermenting social mass, which has since so mightily worked in Upper India, which had long ago operated so powerfully in Europe. War had hitherto formed the trade, the employment, of the rough tribes on the banks of the Jumna: it was now to become their science. A *regular* army was seen for the first time arrayed in the plains of the Upper Doab, across them the earlier flashes of military science broke bright and resistless, and the effect on the politics and tactics of the day was electrical. Wherever Du Boigne and his brigade appeared, wherever the musket and bayonet were opposed to the matchlock and tulwar, Eu-

* Song of Deborah and Barak, Judges, v. 6, 7.

ropean discipline prevailed: Eastern numbers and valour, however great, could make no lasting stand against the science of the West.

Wherever the White Cross of Savoy* flashed across the battle-field victory followed in its train. The heroes of Rajpootana, those bold Rhatores, whose impetuous cavalry had so often swept all

* These were the colours of Du Boigne. To illustrate well the old saying that truth is more wonderful than fiction, we could wish to see a well-written account of the life of this Savoyard adventurer. It would be interesting to watch his career from the time he left his native home at Chamberri, to the day when, with a personal guard of his own, 600 Persian cavalry, he turned his back on Hindostan, of which he had long been the virtual king, to seek that home again. Having served as a soldier under his own prince, then as an ensign in Lord Clare's regiment of the Irish brigade under the French king, later still having fought the Turks in the uniform of the Russian empress, having been imprisoned at Constantinople and sold as a slave, he had gone through all that training of war and adversity which might fit him for the *rôle* he had to play in Hindostan. His parents bought him out of slavery, and he became again an officer in the army of Russia. By one of those seeming chances on which the destinies not only of men but of nations are suspended, Lieutenant Bénit Du Boigne found himself commanding the escort of an English nobleman who was making a progress among the Grecian islands. Lord Percy gave him letters to Warren Hastings, then governor of Bengal, and to Lord Macartney, governor of Madras. After various fortunes, Du Boigne found himself nominally in the service, but in reality master, of Scindia and his domains. And whether as a civil governor or as a military commander, he has left behind him an imperishable name in the north-western provinces of India. (See Mill, book vi. chap. 12, and Mr. Fraser's interesting memoir of Col. Skinner.) As an instance of the terror of Du Boigne's name, we may notice that, when Nujuf Khan, who held the fortress of

before them, even they, at last, were driven off the field, though not without a bloody and terrible resistance.*

Turn the page of History as we may, human nature comes up the same. The first effect of a standing army in the hand of a despot, whether in the Eastern or Western world, is identical; civil

Kanounde, found death approaching, he sent for his begum, and with his dying breath laid this injunction upon her,—" If " Scindia comes make no surrender, but if Du Boigne or Perron " appear, yield at once." Before Du Boigne left India, he was at the head of some forty thousand disciplined troops, with fifty-two pergunnehs east of the Jumna, yielding twenty-two lacs per annum for their maintenance. He had a salary of rs. 6000 a month, besides 2 per cent on the military expenditure. He is described as giant-boned, tall, strong featured, with piercing eyes. From daybreak to midnight he was employed on matters of war, revenue, and diplomacy. The Imperial army, as by favour of the Mogul emperor his force was called, consisted of the following detail:

Six regular brigades, each consisting of 30 battalions of Sepoys and 10 of Nujeebs, 700 men each.

Two thousand regular cavalry and 200 pieces of cannon.

Dowlut Rao Scindia had also a cloud of Mahratta Horse estimated at 100,000, and 2000 irregular infantry.

* On one occasion the irregular beat the disciplined soldiers. See in Skinner's Memoir the account of a charge made by 10,000 Rhatore Rajpoots, who, coming on with a thunder tramp, first at a slow hand-gallop, increasing to the wildest speed, rode through showers of grape and shot, *right over Dudernaig's brigade*, leaving only 200 men on their legs out of 8000; and then, without even looking behind them, rushed upon the Mahratta cavalry of the second line, who, says Skinner, " ran like sheep." A rare instance this of a disciplined force swept down by a herd of irregulars. But the pluck of the Rajpoot has often worked wonders.

subjection is secured, civil liberty is endangered. The change working in Scindia's dominions under Du Boigne in the 18th century, resembled from many points of view the change which France had seen in the 15th century, under Charles VII. or Louis XI., which Spain had seen under Charles V. The sturdy clans of Hindostan, like the nobles of France or the mechanics of Toledo, had to learn the lesson which a regular force alone can teach; they were sinking fast from the state of a warlike nation keeping down a feeble court, to the state of a warlike people kept down by a standing army. If in our own country the civil power was once, though once only, extinguished, when the well-trained dragoons and pikemen of Oliver Cromwell showed our forefathers what discipline could do, we may well believe that the liberty of the subject was a thing of small account, when a Mahratta chieftain first found himself, thanks to a regular army, supreme from the Nerbudda to the Sutlej.

But if History teaches us that a standing army, without a constitutional government, means despotism, we may learn in the same book that a mercenary army, and especially an army commanded by mercenaries, endangers the despot who owns it. What the Swiss hirelings and German black bands were to Europe, the brigades of Du Boigne and Perron were to Upper India. Like other mercenaries, they were good servants, but bad masters; and when Du Boigne, with his sovereign the old Patèl, passed off the scene, Dowlut Rao Scindia found himself in possession of an engine, mighty indeed, yet dangerous to the hands that might attempt to guide or restrain it. At the head of his army was Perron,—the perjured Perron, as the natives of Upper India still call him. Perron hated the English as much as Du Boigne* had respected them, and the flames of war broke out. The ruin which bad policy had begun, bad faith completed. A mercenary traitor admitted, or helped to admit, the soldiers of Lord Lake into the fort of Allyghur, and whilst British arms prevailed on every side, the Mahratta army fast melted into disorder.

It was thus amidst a population swarming with disbanded soldiers, with robbers, with desperadoes, that the earliest English statesmen found themselves legislating for the ceded and conquered provinces of Upper India. The changes from anarchy into subjection which had begun under Du Boigne, had to begin again under Lord Lake. Men are not transformed in a day from freebooting soldiers into orderly subjects. It was long before the old English baron exchanged fighting for politics, before he hung up his sword and dismantled his castle; and though half a century has passed, with scarce a shot fired in the Doab, to this day the husbandman girds on his sword when he passes the boundaries of his own homestead. He has had more leisure for learning the arts of peace than inclination to learn them. But a change, deep though slow, is passing

* It was a saying of Du Boigne's, "Never quarrel with the English."

over the spirit of the people. The splendid barbarity of former ages is fading from their memory, the days of Eastern romance are numbered, the flood of Eastern splendour is receding, but to leave, as we hope, the solid foundations of peace and prosperity behind.

We have dwelt thus upon the historical circumstances which preceded our appearance in Upper India, because they afford a clue whereby to unravel that curious moral tangle, a test whereby to analyse that strange compound of lawlessness, military taste, and civil subjection, which goes to make up the up-country man. We have remarked on other occasions how little these rough sons of nature care for the law, yet how much they respect the lawgiver, or at least the minister of the law; how supremely indifferent they are at once to public peace, and to public liberty. It follows, then, that the difficulties which the ruling power has to encounter in dealing with such a population are peculiar. A liberal Government would gladly encourage public spirit, but its paramount duty is to maintain public order. Press these people too much with rules and restraints, and what chance is there of seeing them free-minded or public-spirited? Take the curb from off them—on the other hand, loosen the reins of government too freely, and what hope is there of public order? In Indian politics, the middle way is the safe way, but it is not an easy way either to find or to keep. Look round the world, and we shall find that in religion, in politics, even in science, great minds only can hold and keep this middle way; it is the acme of modern attainments. But great minds do not grow up like mushrooms, and we have no right to look for them in every Indian Mofussil court. Yet, supposing the mind of the Government to be bent, as we believe it is, on holding this just middle way between severity and indulgence, the men presiding in these courts must interpret and represent that mind to the people of India. However earnestly they strive to do this, their path is beset with snares and difficulties. The daily strife of an Indian magistrate is not so much with *crime* as with *indifference*. He cannot get the people on his side. If he succeed more or less in influencing public opinion in his district, he will fail none the less to awaken public spirit. How, indeed, can any man awaken that which does not even slumber, that of which in Hindostan we can only predicate that it is *not*, not known, not comprehended, not translated, not translateable? To translate the *morale* of M. Curtius, or of Hampden, into Hindostanee, would be as difficult as to mesmerise a crocodile. It is a doctrine for which the Hindoo mind has no room, or, at all events, no place. But public spirit is in other countries the very strongest support to the law and to the magistrate; in England, for instance, when great crime occurs, it prompts every man to track, or if possible to seize, the offender; and what is a magistrate, himself a foreigner and in a foreign land, to do without this great ally? He must do the best he can: not a single friend can he rely upon in India beyond the circle of his own police; and of them there is scarcely one whom he can feel sure of for a single hour. To fight efficiently his daily battle against crime and fraud, the president of an Indian cutcherry requires the spear of Ithuriel, the hands of Briareus, the eyes of Argus; but let him want help as he may, he is all alone, and his pursuit of truth is one endless round of difficulty and disappointment.

We have urged this consideration of the peculiar difficulties to which a magistrate is exposed who has no public to help him, because, without making allowance for this hindrance as well as the other drawbacks which the very history of the people supplies to all administrative efficiency, it would be impossible to weigh justly the merits of the English administration. But, as one crime breeds a second, so does one social defect produce another. Where there is no public spirit there is no very distinct public voice, and where there is no public voice the ruler of the people must often give heed to uncertain sounds. When these sounds come from all sides, and in every variety of discord, he may be tempted to pause, distracted; or if he strike out right or left, he will often strike at random. The Eastern mind loves to throw the honest English understanding into this dilemma. Nothing pleases an astute Hindoo better than the tormenting an enemy *secundum artem* through the instrumentality of a police court. Let him see but a chance of success, and he will rush into the magistrate with cries and gesticulations that must attract attention, and may create sympathy. Self-inflicted wounds, mutilated bodies, false witnesses, all the machinations of perjury and villany, are ready to be brought into play when the opportunity may offer. Hence, whilst his conscience warns the magistrate to listen to every complaint which reaches his ears, his experience must warn him to beware how he listens to, or at all events how he believes, any one of these complaints. An unwilling ear will be closed to cases of real injustice, a too-willing ear will be plied with lies from morning till night. Here, again, discretion, discernment and temper, a clear head and a sound heart, are eminently wanted.

If the evils which we have touched upon be real, —and who that has seen a Mofussil court will deny their reality?—if magistrates in India cannot expect public spirit to come forward and help them, but may expect to find private malignity bent on turning the police courts into instruments of torture, we repeat that it is quite necessary to take these evils, negative and positive, into consideration, if we would rightly appreciate what the career of an Indian magistrate is. The people over whose interests he presides are either rough countrymen, half-robber, half-cultivator or shepherd, servile to his person and office, but supremely indifferent to law, and careless of human life; or they are, as found amongst the towns, a crafty, litigious, lying race, who would use the law as an implement of torture wherewith to ruin or terrify their neighbours. What chance has a magistrate amongst such a people? A warm-hearted, honest Englishman, earnest to improve his district, straining every nerve to hew, if possible, the characters of his people into European form, is like a sculptor cutting an Apollo Belvedere out of sandstone. However firm the hand, however skilful the touch, the work soon crumbles into dust and disappointment.

The best magistrate, then, is he who laughs at disappointment, and works steadily on as though success were still within his reach. And so it is, to a certain degree. It is no small success to win the hearts and affections of a people who, though ignorant or artful, can still be grateful. One thing is very sure, that whatever a magistrate is in India, the people will soon find it out. The native subordinate functionaries watch every turn of his countenance, every inward working of his soul, as a spaniel watches a gamekeeper's whip: the common people watch him as a Persian watches the sun, and regulate their conduct accordingly.

But it is time that we should leave generalities, and come a little to matters of detail. We are not going to inflict, in this place, upon our readers a list of regulations and acts of the Government, but we will invite them to accompany us in what may prove a somewhat desultory search of anything picturesque, interesting, or of practical importance, in up-country police matters. For the use of professional persons who may care to trace the origin of some of our most important rules, we subjoin to this article a few memoranda hastily thrown together, and of no great originality, which still may be interesting to a beginner. (*See* page 199.)

The historian Mill told us long ago, though not

before Bengal had enjoyed many years' experience of Lord Cornwallis's code, that the penal law set up by the English in India was defective in clearness, certainty, promptitude, cheapness, and nice adaptation of penalties to each species of delinquency, to a degree that never had been surpassed and very rarely had been equalled; and added, "Its failure, "therefore, and the misery of the people who must "depend upon it for protection, are not a subject "for surprise."* Now, judging from the documents then before him, we believe the historian was justified in making these severe remarks. But we, writing in the upper provinces, at the present day, are glad to be able conscientiously to declare, that the effects of our penal laws and administration have been beneficial to the people, in, if not the highest, yet a very high degree. The texture of the law is curious enough, if texture be the right term to apply to a piece of patchwork; but if it serves to protect the poor man we will not quarrel with it: a coat may have many colours, and be a very good coat for all that.

One test of the efficiency of the penal law and of its manner of administration, is the prevalence or absence of great crimes. Now, it might not be hard to demonstrate that great crime is less common in Upper India† than in many old settled countries—our own, for instance; and,

* Mill's "History of India," book vi. chap. 6.

† We propose a closer examination of this point in a future number.

at all events, it may be asserted with confidence, that life and property are at this moment generally as secure in the Agra Presidency as in England. To take an example or two. Thuggee, if we are to believe the frequent correspondence of the "Times," is more common in the purlieus of Russell Square than in the metropolis of Upper India. Amongst us in the East, professional villains are to be found occasionally, who, having performed the prescribed ablutions, proceed to drug the traveller for the sake of his money, but it is not in India that wives mix arsenic in their husbands' tea, in order to gain a few pounds by the funeral. The few straggling dacoits of the north-west are not much worse than the many bands of armed burglars in Berkshire or Kent. It is in Surrey, not in Agra, that justices of the peace go to bed with a revolving pistol under their pillow. Highway robbery is far more common on the turnpike roads of Old England, than on the Grand Trunk Road of India.* Bold,

* A late number of the "Times" is on our table, for Monday, July 28th—a busy time, and a time when editors need not beat about for crimes to fill up gaping columns. This paper is full of crime. The Cheshire banditti, with masks and pistols, figure in one page with the Yorkshire highwaymen. Thirteen of these last-named gentry were convicted of highway-robbery at the summer assizes at York, and speaking of this crime, the judge remarked, "that peaceable people walking "about after night-fall were in continual danger of being "attacked and robbed by two or three ruffians banded to- "gether." Is there a district in the Agra Presidency of which the same could be said with truth?

bad men, are common enough in either country; but so long as they stop short of murder, such men run, we believe, a safer career in Great Britain than in Hindostan.

But we may be reminded that petty tyranny and oppression prevail more widely in India than in Europe. We at once reply, that the magistrates sitting in Indian cutcherries are far more ready to put down the tyranny which professional rogues and swindlers practise on the public, than are the magistrates sitting in Bow Street. A man who is swindled out of his money whilst he is awake, has as good a natural right to look to the magistrate for redress, as a man who has been robbed of a sheep or a horse whilst asleep. In England, however, rough sheep or horse-stealers are sent beyond seas, whilst accomplished swindlers live on, unscathed by any magistrate, to prey upon the unsuspecting portion of the public. Frauds, patent to the common sense of all mankind as such, if kept within certain limits well known to their practitioners, are not punishable by a magistrate in England. Similar frauds would bring a delinquent in India at once within the grasp of the law, and the perpetrator would, under the operation of what are called the general regulations, find his way into prison. In illustration of the contrast which in this particular undoubtedly exists between the laws and procedure of the two countries, we offer to our readers the following anecdote, supplied us from the Note-Book of an up-country magistrate. We do not vouch for the legal accuracy of our friend's views, though we can for the literal truth of his story. To our lay mind his reflections seem supported by reason and common sense, but he shall speak for himself.

### *Extract from an Up-country Magistrate's Note-Book.*

*Camp. December* 1850. — I received some papers from one of the deputy-magistrates of my district to-day, which set me thinking whether, after all, justice between man and man is not done as well here as at home. At all events, swindlers and rogues seem to me to thrive in England, and often because the law will not encourage a magistrate to put down fraud and chicanery. Here, on the contrary, every magistrate who has a grain of energy tries to put down fraud, or to punish it, as well as open crime or disorder.

I have fallen into this train of thought owing to the following incident. A few days ago, when taking petitions in the open air, as is my custom, I was struck with the appearance of one of the crowd. He was a well-dressed, venerable-looking old man, with a long silver beard. On to the front of his dress was stuck a petition, well written on an eight anna stamp paper. Both his arms had been cut off, as I afterwards learned, under the native *régime* some fifty years ago, probably on account of some crime. Having lost his arms, the old gentleman had long lived by his wits, and when I saw him was following the vocation of a horse-dealer. I cast my eye over the abstract at the head of the poor creature's petition with interest. It set forth that the petitioner sued under the provisions of Reg. IX. 1807, for restitution of a horse and some clothes taken from him by force. In the body of the petition it was stated that the petitioner (Syed Ali by name) had taken a horse valued at Rs. 500 to the great fair at Butesur for sale: that the said horse having fallen sick, Rambux had offered to take it to his village and cure it: that the animal was taken accordingly to Rambux's home, and there doctored: that when the petitioner wanted to take away his horse, the defendant Rambux threatened to assault him, and seized the animal, and his clothes worth Rs. 5. That the petitioner, being a poor helpless traveller, came straight to the magistrate to claim protection and assistance. The person against whom the complaint lay was a zemindar of my district, of decent repute, and I did not believe that he had done anything very criminal, but as his village was near the tehseel station, I referred the petitioner to the tehseeldar, and directed that functionary, who was a deputy-magistrate, to see justice done to him.

I soon got the papers of the case from the deputy, who reported that Syed Ali had applied to the defendant Rambux to cure his horse, that Rambux had agreed to do so on condition that if the animal, which was in a very bad way, recovered, he, Rambux, was to get one-third of the price it might fetch in the fair; in which case all expenses of food and medicines would be defrayed by the horse-doctor. A written agreement to this effect had been drawn up, and taken at the instance of the Syed to the police-office to be attested. That the deputy-magistrate had seen the horse, which was still ailing, and that Rambux refused to let the owner take away the horse before the cure was complete, until the expenses of food and medicine had been paid, and a loan of Rs. 5, cash advanced to the Syed, repaid.

My order on receiving this report was, that if the horse-dealer wanted redress he might apply to the civil courts, as the case was clearly not a criminal one; but I added, as the defendant in the case was a respectable man, I doubted not that if the Syed would pay expenses, and repay the loan made to him, the horse would be given up. I have just heard that both parties took my advice, and so the matter is settled. Now, it may or may not be desirable that, as a general rule, magistrates should interfere, as I and my deputy did in this case; yet, on the whole, I contend, that the spirit of readiness to listen at all events to men who complain of injury, is one that should be encouraged. There is little fear of too much being done; the natural desire of most public men is to avoid labour which does not legitimately belong to them, and they have more reason to fear the temptation to do too little than the inducements to do too much. I should never have noted down so commonplace a transaction as that between Syed Ali and Rambux but for the contrast which it displays, so far as the magisterial animus is concerned, to another affair about a horse which lately came to my notice when I was on furlough at home.

I was living a few miles out of London, in Essex. One morning I came up by the coach, for we still have coaches from our village to the city, and got into an omnibus in Bishopsgate Street to go the West End. Before we had passed Cornhill, a gentleman, somewhat flurried in his manner, got hastily in, and as we drove on I recognised in the new passenger an old Hayleybury acquaintance, whom I had not seen since we both left College some fifteen years back. After mutual exclamations of pleasure at the meeting, my friend informed me that he had been swindled out of *35l.* that morning, and was in, what is vulgarly called, a *fix*, not knowing how to retrieve a false step which he had made.

Thus ran his story. "You know I have just come home on furlough. I was in want of a hunter, and came up from the country this morning to look at a 'genuine mare' advertised for sale, price fifty-five guineas, the property of a gentleman who might be spoken to. The mare was standing at a Mews, near Baker Street. Here I found a smart groom, who said, 'Master's' name was John Sharp, Esquire, that he was staying at an hotel in the neighbourhood, and added, 'I'll step over and fetch him.'"

"John Sharp, Esquire, soon made his appearance, a fresh-looking man, with a sharp, brown eye, a bottle-green cut-away coat, drab trousers, red neckcloth, with a look of quiet, suppressed slang about him, which ought to have put me on my guard. Pulling a key out of his pocket, he opened the stable door, and showed me the hunter. Liking the look of the mare I asked for a trial, to which the owner at once assented. Tom the groom saddled her, and led her out into the yard. I was just about to put my foot in the stirrup, when Mr. Sharp came forward, and said, 'No offence, Sir, I am sure you are quite the gentleman, and that everything is all right, but, as I have not the pleasure of knowing you, just as a matter of business I'll trouble you for a deposit.' Seeing me hesitate, he went on, 'a mere form, Sir; a cheque will do, Sir, if you do not happen to have the cash about you.' Well, to make a long story short, I gave Mr. Sharp a cheque on my bankers for 35*l.*, tried the mare, found that she went *tender* before, and she was broken-winded, and in a few minutes returned to the Mews. Tom ran out to hold the mare, and the moment I was off her back, led her into the stable, and locked the door. I felt a twinge of insecurity, as Tom came up with a touch of the hat, and began, 'Well, Sir, how do you find her? Werry tidy mare we reckons her, and Master wouldn't a part with her, hever so, only he's been a going—excuse me, Sir—rayther too fast lately, and is a breaking up of his stablishment.'

"I suggested that the mare was lame and broken-winded.

*Tom.*—"'Well, Sir, she *be* a little shade thick in the wind, but, bless you, Sir, that's no deturment;—but I'll run and call Master, you ad better speak to him.' Exit Tom, leaving me outside the stable door, tapping my boot, biting my lips, and watching a pecuniary transaction in progress at the next stable-door between a coachman's wife and a costermonger. For a weary half-hour did I stand sentry over that stable-door, until at last Tom appeared again, munching an apple very leisurely.

"'Where is your Master?' I said, angrily enough.

*Tom.*—"'Well, Sir, Master has stepped out; but he's left word I was to take the balanst of the fifty-five guineas, if you wished to take the mare.'

"'But,' thundered I, 'if I don't want to take the mare, what then?'

*Tom.*—"'Well, Sir, *then* you'd better speak to Master; all I know is you must pay money down before I unlocks that ere door. Master is a werry partickler gentlmun, and I darn't give you the mare without the money. It ud be as much as my place is worth.'

"'Where is your Master?' I asked once more.

*Tom.*—"'Well, Sir, I bleive he's gone into the country: a party called for him whilst you was on the mare.'

"I felt that I was *done*, jumped into a cab, hurried to my bankers, found the cheque had been cashed, and Mr. Sharp was *nowhere*.

"Running over with indignation, I hurried to the Police-office in —— Street, and made my way into the presence of the sitting magistrate, who was lounging over the 'Morning Post.' I began my story ;—when I had got half through it, the magistrate looked surlily up from his paper, took a contemptuous stare at me, (my friend was as well dressed and good-looking a man as one could meet), and then drawled out,—as he turned over the leaves of the 'Post,' 'Go out, will you, and don't take up the time of the court with your nonsense.'

"I left the place in disgust, and, fool though I have been, I still rejoice to think that, at all events, I never treated the poorest native in the way this London magistrate treated me. I have been to consult a friend at the India House, and am now on my way back to the stables."

Here ended my friend's story.

Although I thought his position rather hopeless so far as the *35l.* was concerned, I suggested an interview with my solicitor; but on hearing the case, the man of law at once pronounced that the only resource was a civil action, but that we should not find Mr. Sharp "worth powder and shot."

And thus rogues prey upon the unsuspecting portion of mankind in England every day in the year. As an illustration of the popular feeling in such cases, I will quote the remark of my friend the coachman of our coach. He could not restrain a grin as I went over my friend's story. "Well, "Sir," he said, "excuse me; but the gent was to be "sure raything in a manner of speaking what we "calls softish; howsomedever that knowing cove "would not a treated *me* so, he'd a knowed better. "Bless your heart I'd a been the death on him, I'd "a watched for him, I'd a waited for him, if it had "been a twelvemonth, and I'd a *punched his ed* "against a lamp-post!"

Now I have only to say, that had the scene of Mr. Sharp's proceedings been at my station of Jungle-poor, instead of in Baker Street, and had I been informed of them by a credible person, I would have done my best to lay hold of such a rascal, and supposing the case proved against him, the taking money on false pretences and then making off with it, I would have put Mr. Sharp on the roads. I also believe that the Sessions Judge, who knows the law of our Courts as well as any man living, would have supported my decision on appeal.

Having given our friend's story, we shall satisfy ourselves for the present with bringing forward one other instance of the superiority, in certain cases, of the criminal law as administered in India, over the criminal law of Great Britain, not indeed as regards the letter of the statute, but as to rules and mode of practice.

When a young Englishman fresh from College takes his seat for the first time, as an assistant to the magistrate of an Indian district, one of the many puzzling technical terms which he meets with is the word *budmāash.* If our tyro be a sensible youth, and not ashamed of his ignorance, he asks what the word means; if he is foolish enough to hope that he can hide his lingual deficiencies from the *omlah,* as sharp a set as the world can produce, he notes the expression, and looks it out at home in his dictionary. He then learns that *bud* means bad, and *māash* means livelihood, and that the term '*badmāash*' is applicable to persons of bad repute, who have no ostensible means of earning an honest livelihood.

If a man leads an idle dissolute life, and is notorious as a thief or a vagabond, it is the duty of the magistrate in India, on being duly certified to the above effect, to call the accused person before him, and institute an inquiry into his way of life. Habitual offenders against the law are at once directed to furnish security for their good conduct, and failing to do so, are sent to prison, either for a year, by order of the magistrate, or for as much as three years, by the Sessions Court, if their case may seem to require such precautionary treatment. Without this power, the authorities would never have been able to introduce that degree of order and public peace for which the Upper Provinces of India are generally remarkable.

In England, notwithstanding the existence of a statute* which might be enforced with the best

* Here is the opinion of a jurist of no mean repute in England, Mr. M. D. Hill, Q. C., Recorder of Birmingham :—

" There is a statute on the books," says Mr. Hill, " by which a reputed or suspected thief, by frequenting streets and certain places therein described, which are supposed to furnish greater opportunities for plunder than others, may, if the magistrate before whom he is brought infer from such frequenting that his intent was to commit a felony, be adjudged to be a rogue, and may be punished with imprisonment.

" What I would propose is, that when, by the evidence of two or more credible witnesses, a jury has been satisfied that

effect, notwithstanding the dire want of some such safety-valve, the magistrates are unable to rid the streets of the swarms of notorious thieves, shop-lifters, and pick-pockets, who infest the larger cities. None of our readers need to be told, that in our otherwise happy Isle there exists a class of men, boys, and children, distinct even in their physical characteristics from the industrious million, a class banded together almost from infancy against the peace, property, and morality of their country. Bred in cellars, and dens of infamy, educated in the streets, lodging in slums, or in any corner out of sight of the policeman, grow up amidst profligacy, debauchery, and crime, "*les classes dangereuses*" of our English society. Fearing neither God nor devil, hating and hated, these human harpies exist only by preying upon their kind. Professional plunderers, such as these, are just as well known to the police, as the police are known to them. We lament the sad fate which thus trains up responsible beings to certain crime and dishonor, but we also lament that the opportunities of such training are allowed. Moral lepers should be treated as men

there is good ground for believing, and that the witnesses do actually believe, that the accused party is addicted to robbery or theft, so as to deserve the appellation of 'thief,' he shall be called upon in defence to prove himself in possession of means of subsistence, lawfully obtained, either from his property, his labour, or from the assistance of his friends. On the failure of such proof, let him be adjudged a reputed thief, and put under high recognizances to be of good conduct for some limited period; or, in default of responsible bail, let him suffer imprisonment for the same term."

afflicted with physical pestilence, should be tended, watched, and cured; and then, but not till then, sent into the world of every-day life. Infection, at all events, should be prevented, and in India it is so prevented, where a confirmed "*mauvais sujet*" is taken up, put into prison, and taught to make carpets or paper, or set to work on the public roads. Are we wrong in saying that here again Indian mofussil law has the advantage?

We hope that the comparisons which we have attempted to draw will not be misunderstood, as though we put them forward in the wretched "*tu quoque*" spirit of argumentation, which tries to puff up one cause by running down another. Our mofussil police and magisterial courts have, we well know, many faults to which we hope hereafter to direct attention; but there are also in our criminal procedures some strong redeeming points, marked by practical usefulness and sound common sense. Let us give credit where credit is due. We have still much to contend with, why should we fear to assert that much has been accomplished?

---

## Memorandum on the Rise and Progress of Criminal Law in the Bengal Presidency.

(*See* page 185.)

Before we can attempt to sketch the outline of our up-country penal code, it will be necessary to examine its origin. The body of laws introduced into the ceded and conquered Provinces has, for its prototype, Lord Cornwallis's Bengal Code of 1793. On the present occasion we shall satisfy ourselves with running "*currente calamo*" over those earlier rules on which our existing Regulations are founded. Nor will our limits allow us in this paper to get beyond the laws introduced into the Benares Province in 1795.

The Bengal Code may be traced back to the "General Regulations for the Administration of Justice" proposed by the Committee of Circuit at Cossim-bazaar, and "made and ordained by the President and Council in Bengal in 1772."

From this date the Collector of each district was not only to preside in the Provincial Court of Dewannee, on the part of the Company (in their quality of "King's Dewan"), but also was to attend to and watch the proceedings of the Foujdarree Adawlut. The sword of the magistrate was at this time ostensibly wielded by the Nazim, or supreme magistrate, whose authority was derived, or supposed to be derived, from the imperial fountain of law and dominion at Delhi. The *real* power was generally in the hands of Warren Hastings. The besetting sin of this great man, which was to bring upon him, ten years later, the thundering vituperation of Burke before the Commons, and which, five years after that, was to put him on his knees in Westminster Hall before the Peers of England, the sin of "*unscrupulousness*," breaks out in his Minutes at this early date.

Dacoits were the scourge of Bengal then as they are now, and by the 35th article of the new Regulations such offenders were declared liable to capital punishment, whilst their families were to be condemned to *perpetual slavery*. The Committee had apologised for proposing this severe enactment, but Hastings, in a letter (signed by him as President of Council, 10th July, 1773), not only defended this harsh law, but also urged the necessity of selling as slaves, or transporting in slavery to Fort Marlborough, *all convicted felons* and life prisoners. "By "this means," he says, "the Government will be released from "a heavy expense in erecting prisons, keeping guards in monthly "pay, and in the maintenance of accumulated crowds of pri-"soners. The sale of the convicts will raise a considerable "fund if these disorders continue. If not, the effect will be yet "more beneficial."

To support these severe propositions, he states that the Mahometan law is founded on the most lenient principles, and an abhorrence of blood, whilst the instances of strict and exemplary justice done by Mahometan princes, and recorded in history, are of the most sanguinary kind, and inflicted *without regard to law;* whence he argues it is necessary and desirable for the sovereign power to depart, in extraordinary cases, from the strict letter of the law; and he recommends this practice to his brother counsellors. Thus did the dispenser of law trample law under foot.

The evil of false complaints to which we have adverted in our preceding article, seems to have been common, and a very wholesome rule was made, which, with certain limitations, would be useful in the present day. In the 16th Article of the Regulations of 1772, the custom of levying *chowt*, or other fee or commission on the account of money recovered, or *etlāk*, a fine on the decision of causes, as well as all heavy arbitrary fines (in civil suits), is abolished. "But," says Article 17th, "as "cases may occur, in which it will be highly necessary for the "welfare of the community, to curb and restrain trivial and "groundless complaints, and to deter chicane and intrigue; "which passions amongst these people *often work to the undoing of their neighbours;* a discretion shall, in such cases, be left "to the court, either to impose a fine, not exceeding five Rupees, "or inflict corporal punishment not exceeding twenty lashes with "a rattan, according to the degree of the offence and the person's "station in life." We think that in the present day a few rattans would operate well in such cases, and deter people from resorting to the courts of justice in order to oppress their enemies, or to extort money from the public more effectually than fine or imprisonment, which our existing laws adjudge in such cases. In the civil courts especially the revival of some such enactment as this would work like a charm, for there are persons who use these courts as wicked priests once used the Inquisition, and who hold the threat of a civil suit, to be supported by forged documents and false swearing, as an Italian bandit holds a blunderbuss to the head of a wealthy traveller. And, to tell the truth, the public in some parts of India where forgers and false swearers have long triumphed, no more desire to find themselves as defendants in a civil suit opposed to such machinators, than the good people of the sixteenth century desired to find themselves handed over to the civil power on the prosecution of the Courts Spiritual.

But this is a digression, and probably an unprofitable one, as it is, we fear, too late to hope that our civil courts will burst forth from the time-honoured cerements of law and form, to administer speedy and substantial justice. We now take leave of the Code of 1773, with the remark that in it we may trace the germ of most of our subsequent legislation.

In 1774 we find Hastings appointing thannah, or police stations, and stung to the quick apparently by the continued ravages of dacoits, urging that "all persons of whatever degree " or profession who shall be convicted of receiving fees or other " pecuniary acknowledgments from robbers, knowing them to " be such, or of abetting or conniving in any shape in their " practices, shall be adjudged equally criminal with them, and " punished with death." At the same time he revived the old offices of foujdar and thannadar. (See extracts from the proceedings of the Governor and Council, under date 19th April, 1774, quoted by Colebrooke in his Supplement to the Digest of Regulations and Laws.)

By the resolutions of Government, recorded on the 6th April, 1781, the foujdars and thannadars were recalled, the judges of the several Dewannee Adawluts were invested with the power of magistrates for the apprehending of daçoits, though the power of punishing such delinquents was still reserved to the Courts of Nizamut Adawlut acting in the name of the Nabob. And, in order to lick the criminal statements and police reports of all these odd courts into shape, a covenanted officer was appointed on a salary of Rs. 1000 per mensem, with the title of "Remembrancer of the Criminal Courts." At this period we have only to remark, that the general spirit of the legislation was of a practical turn; that the English officers, under the cloak of the Nabob's name, exercised great power in a somewhat unscrupulous manner; and that, notwithstanding Hastings' remarks on the bloodless character of the Mahometan law, wretches used, by its operation, even under the eye of the English courts, to suffer amputation of one or more limbs for grave offences.

Passing on to 1787, we then find the district chief as judge, collector, and magistrate, deciding petty cases and inspecting jails. Still, however, the larger share of criminal authority remained nominally with the Nabob, Mahomed Reza Khan, in his capacity of Naib Nazim.

Three years later, owing to the "numerous robberies, murders, and other enormities daily committed throughout the country," and for other weighty reasons, we find further changes required. The jurisdiction of the judge—collector sitting as magistrate was defined, the curtain dropped upon the Naib Nazim, and the Governor-general, Lord Cornwallis, stood forth and expressed his determination to *resume* the superintendence of the administration of criminal justice throughout the British Provinces. Four courts of circuit, three for Bengal and one for the Behar Province, were established. Two convenanted Civil Servants of the Company sat in these courts, assisted by a Cazee and Muftee. The chief criminal court, or Nazamut Adawlut, was removed from Moorshedabad to Calcutta, and the Governor-general and Members of Council presided, with the head Cazee of the provinces, and two Muftees, to expound the law when wanted. The decisions of this high court were under certain restrictions to be regulated by the Mahometan law. By these restrictions the absurd distinctions made by Aboo Huneefah as to the mode of the commission of murder, were set aside, and the relations of the murdered man were no longer to be permitted to pardon the offender and stand between the law and the law's victim.

It was not till 1791 that the Governor-general in Council resolved that the punishment of mutilation should be discontinued. The loss of one limb was to be exchanged for seven years' imprisonment with labour, and loss of two limbs for fourteen years' similar punishment.

In the following year it was ordered that the police establishments hitherto kept up by landholders in virtue of their engagements to Government should be discharged, and police officers in future should be nominated by the magistrate. The darogha of police thus commissioned was ordered, amongst other duties, to apprehend and send to the magistrate all vagrants or suspected persons who might be lurking about his jurisdiction without any ostensible means of subsistence, or who could not give a satisfactory account of themselves. Here we may trace the origin of the future "*bud-māash*" regulations, of which notice has been made in the article to which this Memorandum belongs. The village watchmen, those useful links in the great police chain—that is to say, useful when well paid and looked after—were put under the darogha's control. Police dâks were established, and certain piratical-shaped boats were put under an interdict. Most of these rules were well adapted to the existing state of things.

And now, in 1793, legislation was attempted on a more ambitious scale. Lord Cornwallis decided to separate the collector's office from that of the magistrate and judge. This was good European policy, but, in our opinion, not suited to the latitude of Bengal ;)and our own private belief (a weakness, it may be) is, that if one district chief, within moderate limits, had remained supreme in each Bengal district, we should not hear so much of dacoits and gang-robbers along the lower Ganges as we now do. But we are wandering from our subject, and will only make one more remark on the complicated and tedious enactments of 1793. These laws contain three elements, English justice, English common sense, and English law. For the justice and common sense which pervade the Code, we give Lord Cornwallis our best thanks; never were such wholesome infusions more welcome. For the English law, we beg to say, that it is all very good in its way for those who like it, in her Majesty's Courts at Westminster, but it never did any good, and never will do any good in Bengal. What European *fire-water* has been physically to the Red Indian, European law has been morally to the Indians of the East. Millions of simple men, alike in the Lower and Upper Provinces, curse the day when they or their fathers first tasted English law, so far as it is developed in our civil jurisprudence; under its forms and delays thousands of village communities, which neither force nor famine could disperse, have crumbled into dust.

But, we must hasten on, and will ask our readers only to pause a moment with us at our own classic city of Benares, to take one taste of English law made expressly for the Brahmins of the place—a race of men, like Corporal Bunting's cat, more feared than respected. Class legislation, as it is called, is bad enough under any circumstances, but when bad laws are made to save bad men from punishment, the extreme of legal absurdity would seem to have been attained. But, no; any man may learn how bad laws, such as these, can be made worse, by legal forms and technicalities, and to any sceptic we beg to suggest a careful perusal of Reg. 21 of 1795. This law provides for the punishment of Brahmins in Benares. Amongst them an accursed practice used to prevail of threatening to kill themselves, and, what was much worse, their wives and children, when anything contrary to their wishes was required of them. Such sacrifices of wives and little ones by fire or the sword were by no means uncommon, and as Brahmins, do what crime they might, were not to be subjected to capital punishment, some law was considered necessary to meet these atrocious cases. Benares happened to have been under a Hindoo ruler before Warren Hastings laid hands on the province, but let us suppose, for argument's sake, that the Brahmins of Benares had, under any of the more reputable Mahometan princes, commenced sacrificing their children when the tax-gatherer came to their doors; the Mahometan would have had blood for blood, and the Brahmin would at once have expiated his unnatural crime with his life. But when once the taste for English legal forms, delays, and observances had come in, summary punishment, however just, was out of the question. Besides the sort of benefit of clergy, which the laws extended to all Brahmins in Benares, the very forms of those laws put summary punishment, and even summary repression of crime, out of the question.

The tehsildar, let us suppose, had intended to enforce through a peon the ordinary process of the revenue authorities to realise money due by a land-holding Brahmin. The Brahmin bars his outer door, and declares his intention to establish a *koorh;* in other words, catches hold of a knife or a torch in one hand, of his infant child in the other, and vows to burn or slay if he is asked to pay a single rupee. Now, observe the process according to law, whilst the Brahmin is killing his family,—

1st.—The peon is to wait upon the tehsildar.

2d.—Tehsildar (after taking peon's deposition) to wait upon the collector.

3d.—Collector to summon the Government vakeel.

4th.—Government vakeel to move the magistrate.

5th.—Magistrate to send a relative to the angry Brahmin.

6th.—Relative failing "*componere lites*," then a *Brahmin* Chuprassey was to enter upon the negotiation.

7th.—*Brahmin* failing, a *Mahometan* peon was to take the offender into custody, if he could catch him.

Lastly.—If the Mahometan peon arrived too late, and found only the ashes or the mangled bodies of the Brahmin's family, then the Brahmin himself, when caught, would be liable to transportation, and his family (such as survived) were to be banished, and their lands forfeited. So the families of such Brahmins as had a bad temper, and a dislike to cash payments, had the option of being burnt or being banished!

Such of our readers as are blessed with children round their knees will recognise in this animated series of legal proceedings enumerated above, the original of that popular nursery myth, in which the prominent characters are an old woman and a pig. "Water won't quench fire, fire won't burn stick, stick won't beat dog, dog won't bite pig, pig won't get over gate, and I shan't get home to my supper to-night."

Thank Heaven, we have got rid of most of these forms in our criminal and revenue institutions; but *they cluster thick around the temple of civil justice still.* And here, having worked our way home to Benares, we must pause, with the hope of carrying this hurried examination of the law, further up the country in our next number.

# VII.

## NOTES ON THE POLICE.

---

THEMISTOCLES, when desired at a feast to touch the lute, replied, "I cannot fiddle, but I can make of a small town a great city." Now, for India we want, if we can get them, men who shall come up to the vaunt of the Athenian commander; not fiddlers, but men of pith and progress. We look for science, not art; statesmen, not lawyers; above all, for our magistrates we require officers possessing nerve, action, and energy. For Governors, Councillors, and Judges, we may hope to find statesmen of patient inquiry and investigation, in whom thought predominates over action. But, for our magistrates in India, we demand the graces which (if we may fetch another simile from Athens) Demosthenes required in an orator. First, Action. Second, Action. Third, Action. And if to action be joined that great though rare gift of *moral thoughtfulness*, so valuable to the man of power and movement, these qualities combined with a fair share of ability and judgment will give us all we could ask, and more than we shall often get for our public men. The more a magistrate has these characteristics, and the more equally they are diffused over his character, the better he will be.

Action, however, and energy, are what we now lay most stress upon, because in days of peace and outward tranquillity these qualities are not always valued at their true price, and their absence is not so palpably mischievous as in more stirring times. There is more danger now of men becoming plodding, methodical, mere office functionaries, than of their stepping with too hasty a zeal beyond the limits of the law. There is truth, too, in Jacquemont's sneer—India *is* governed by stationery, to a more than sufficient extent; and one of the commonest errors of our magistrates, which they imbibe from constant and early Indian associations, is to mistake *writing* for *action*, to fancy that *dictation* will supply the place of *exertion*. In no other country are so many written orders issued with so much confidence, received with such respect, and broken with such complacency. In fact, as for writing, we believe the infection of the "*cacoethes scribendi*" must first have grown up in the East. It pervades everything, but is more rampant and more out of place in a police-office than anywhere else.* It was not the ma-

* We do not mean to undervalue the daily written police reports, which are of the greatest importance; what we protest against is, the needless spinning out of these daily advices, and

gistrates who originated this passion for scribbling, but they have never succeeded in repressing it, nor, whilst the law requires that every discontented old woman's story shall be taken down in writing, is it to be expected they ever will. The Khayeths worship their pen and ink on certain festivals, and there is a sort of "*religio*" attaching to written forms and statements which is not confined to official life, but pervades the whole social polity of the writing tribes. An Indian scribe, whose domestic expenditure may average sixpence a-day, will keep an account-book with as many columns, headings, and totals, as would serve for the budget of a Chancellor of the Exchequer.* To Tudor Mul and such worthies we owe, no doubt, a great deal for the method and order which they infused into public records; but we have also to thank these knights of the pen for the plaguiest long-figured statements, and the greatest number of such statements, which the world ever saw.

the filling them with useless matter. It is amusing to watch a native officer—a deputy-magistrate, for instance—on whom, once in a way, the duty of disposing of the police reports for the day is devolved. He invariably thinks it his business to pass some sort of order on every item of the thanadar's day-book, and if no other remark can be made, puts "*has been read*" opposite the most trifling entry.

* It is remarkable that the Hindoos keep no written accounts in the shape of what we call history, nor even such memoranda as can furnish material for the historian, whilst they preserve the minutest details of everything connected with national revenue or expenditure. *See* MALCOLM'S *Central India*, vol. i. p. 58–60.

If, then, the genius of the people lead them to mistake writing for action, we need not wonder if the servants of Government imbibe more or less the same dangerous error. That such is the genius of the people we need hardly stop to prove. Take an instance from every-day life. A man succeeds to the management of landed property, and deputes an agent to look after it. An English agent under such circumstances would get on his pony, and ride over every part of the estate. An Indian *homme d'affaires* squats in the most comfortable place he can find, and prepares, at second hand, an interminable detail of every field, &c. &c. The one would do and see much but write little, the other sees nothing and does nothing but write volumes. Hence in India we want an accountant for every village, hence the need for every petty chief to entertain almost as many penmen as ploughmen. Our laws, as we have already hinted, favour this Eastern weakness; if two neighbours quarrel about a drain or a dunghill, a rough word or a hasty blow, their mutual recriminations must all be taken down in black and white, with the statements of all their witnesses, before the smallest legal sentence can be passed. This process is requisite, not only in cases appealable to the higher courts, but also in the pettiest causes in which the order of the magistrate is final. Tons of paper pass daily into the criminal record-rooms, filled with the most trivial occurrences, described with the greatest possible minuteness.

Such being the "*idola specus*" which haunt.

the earliest steps of Indian officials, and such the tendency of the public mind, we need not wonder that the personal prowess, energy, and activity displayed by men of rank have held a high, perhaps an undue place, in the estimation of the people. Men accustomed to see all official labour pushed off upon deputies, and to consider power synonymous with ease and luxury, are delighted with a district chief who is as ready to spend the day in the saddle, if need be, as in the cutcherry.

Men admire most what they least understand. Napoleon, when he wished to make the greatest impression on his officers, put on the cap of the *savant* and solved problems with the sages of "the Institute." In like manner, a magistrate, who will ride sixty miles across country, if need require, will at once secure the respect of his satraps and the votes of his people. The gallant bearing of William Frazer, at the head of his squadron of horse, is still the talk of the men of Delhi: the rough Jats and Goojurs, in the valleys of the lower Himaleyeh, still tell their children how Frederick Shore cut down in single combat the best swordsman of the Upper Doab. But even amongst ordinary men, in ordinary times, there is not seldom a demand for promptitude in action and presence of mind, which makes no unimportant part of the schooling of our Indian statesmen. In turning over the pages of the "Note-Book," to which we have been on former occasions indebted, we have come upon the following description, which we transcribe. It seems to us to afford an illustration of the activity which on occasion is required from a magistrate in India. Our readers will recognise in the "Mr. Clerk" alluded to, the present Sir George, late Governor of Bombay.

## Cutcherry on Horseback.

### *From a Magistrate's Note-Book.*

In the year 1835 I was an assistant to the magistrate of Paneeput, and was stationed at the then flourishing cantonment of Kurnal. I had charge of that place, and of two or three of the thanas near it. My master, John Lawrence, loved then as now to encourage a spirit of action and energy in his subordinates, and his name was as much respected then amongst the Jats, Goojurs, and Ranghurs of the Jumna, as it now is amongst the Bunnoochees, Wuzeerees, or other wild tribes on the Indus. One morning in November I was sitting in my tent, doing cutcherry, as the phrase goes, when two travel-stained men pushed in and asked to speak to me in private. No sooner was the tent cleared than one of my visitors, after glancing around, unloosed his waistband, and pulled out of its folds a note from the "*burra sahib,*" as he said. It was from George Clerk, the political agent at Umballah in those days, and from its contents I learned, that certain freebooters of my district, with the help of some of the men of Khytul (a protected Sikh state), had made a raid upon the village of Asynduh, near Umballah, and had carried off a large herd of cattle at the point of the spear, killing or wounding whoever opposed them. The messengers were the Jat headmen of Asynduh, owners of the lost cattle, and the killed and wounded villagers were their relations and dependants.

I fancy now I can see the dusky faces of these injured men, burning with rage and revenge, and feel their hot breath as they whispered to me how, where, and when I was to help them to recover, at all events, their property, if not more fully to avenge their wrongs. Above a whisper I could not persuade them to speak, though nobody was within a stone's throw of the tent. From their story it seemed that the men of my district, who had helped the Khytul marauders, were afraid to keep any of the harried cattle in the Paneeput villages, and that the greater part of the buffaloes were at a village called Ooblana, in the Khytul state, some twenty odd miles from Kurnal. From fear of detection, the herds were kept day and night in the dense jungles near the village, and only brought morning and evening to a tank under the village walls to be milked. The Jats urged me, on a fixed day, to bring out a party of horsemen, when they promised to meet me at daybreak near Ooblana, and point out, if not the thieves, at all events the lost cattle. Above all things, I was to give no hint of my intentions to any living man, or the expedition would be a failure.

On the night preceding the day fixed for my "*dour*," on going to bed I told my bearer to wake me about midnight. I then rode off with the thanadar of Kurnal and as many sowars as I could muster (about eleven in all), taking the road to Ooblana. I ordered the vakeel of Khytul to attend me,—a fat, jolly little man, called Dewan Singh, who rode a capital Tangun pony. The animal, over-fed, under-worked, and excited by the number of horses about him, jumped and kicked more than was agreeable to his master, to the great amusement of the sowars, who kept cutting their jokes at the expense of the sleek Dewan. "Wah, wah," "*keisa buboola Ghora*, what a fly-away steed!" they cried; "bravo, "vukeel sahib; you'll catch all the dacoits be-"fore we can come up if you go on at that pace."

Somewhat incautiously, I mentioned to the vakeel that his services would be required at Ooblana to make an impression upon the head men of the place, who had been cattle-lifting. He promised to do his best, but doubted if the people would listen to him; though, he added, possibly the thanadar might who lived in the town. About a coss from Ooblana I met one of the Jat head men, who ran on to show the way. My horse, glad to move faster through the chilly morning air, broke into a hand-gallop, and when I pulled up to let the guide come on, the fat vakeel was reported missing. His horse had last been seen running off towards home with him, through the grass jungle, at a pace which the sowars declared it was no wish of the rider to encourage. From this I understood that Dewan

Singh had no taste for a controversy with the men of Ooblana, and, when I knew more of them, I thought him quite right.

The sun was just rising over the broad leaves of the Dhāk jungle bushes, when my guide pointed to a mango tree, from which came down two of his party, and informed us that the buffalo herd was close by. We pushed on, the tall wiry Jats running like antelopes as we got near the milking-place. From a rising knoll I could see some hundred buffaloes standing quietly round one of the sedgy pools, which in those parts are found here and there amongst the bush-jungle. Three or four men, armed only with light hatchets, were watching them. And now we came in sight of the village, or town rather, of red brick, with a wall round it, and strong gateway, the land near being cultivated as far as a matchlock could carry from the wall, and no further. Beyond, all was thick grass and bush-jungle. The Jats, rushing in amongst the cattle, soon tied the arms of the astonished herdsmen, and joyfully recognised several of their lost buffaloes.

A few minutes had passed in counting and examining the animals, which seemed to know the voice of their owners, when all at once a cry came sweeping down the west wind, so loud and so shrill as to make the old woods round us ring again. "Hark!" said my men; "there is the '*Rooka*:' we shall soon have the villagers down upon us." Hastily ordering the sowars to keep the buffaloes well together, I pushed on towards the town. A chuprassey, mounted on a horse of mine, and the Kurnal thanadar, both of whom I knew to be courageous men, followed me. "Look, sir," said the thanadar, "look at the rascals coming down "like ants out of that fort, and then, perhaps, "you will understand why I do not fancy coming "on these *dours* alone; if your honour were not "here, do you suppose those cut-throats would let "one of us escape alive?" Whilst he yet spoke the enemy were upon us; lines of rough-looking fellows, armed, some with spears, some with matchlocks, blowing away at their matches, some with big clubs only, came sallying out of the town-gate, whilst the walls above and around were crowded with old men, women, and children, all screeching like so many jackals. Conceive the cry of a pack of fox-hounds joined to a chorus of Indian watchmen and pariah dogs, and you will have only some faint idea of what the "*Rookuh*," or war-cry of a Ranghur village is. My chuprassey, riding up to the foremost man, called out, "Stop, rascal! don't you see the Sahib Buhadoor?" He might as well have spoken to the wind. I tried to stop the next man by pulling a pistol out of my holsters, and pointing it in his face. He coolly said, "Shoot away, if you like, but you won't get our buffaloes," and then ran off after the next towards the pool. At this moment I recollected what the fat vakeel had told me about there being a thana at Ooblana, and pushed through the gate, determined to call the Sikh thanadar to account. I did not know then, what I afterwards learned, that this worthy official was the very man who had plotted the raid on Asynduh, and was to have netted the biggest share of the booty, if I had not come to disturb his arrangements. I had some difficulty in getting by the crowds of armed men in the narrow street, but, sticking the spurs into my horse, forced my way on as well as I could. Before I had reached the thana I met the thanadar, with two other horsemen — fine, handsome, well-armed Sikhs, all three were, and ready for mischief they looked — charging down the street, whilst the people *salaamed* to them right and left. On seeing my white face, the thanadar's jaw fell, as, putting my hand into my pocket, I exclaimed, "Here is Mr. Clerk's letter: I am his friend; if one of *my* buffaloes is carried away by these vagabonds Mr. Clerk will hang you over your own gate."

I turned my horse's head, and then, calling on the thanadar to follow, proceeded towards the buffalo pool. The men of Ooblana had been too many for my troopers, and had carried the cattle off into the jungles, out of sight or hearing. Here and there a straggling horseman came sneaking out of the thicket, looking foolish and disconcerted. I vowed to the thanadar that I would never leave the place without my buffaloes, and that he should be held responsible for the consequences if they were not restored to me. We galloped off in the direction from which our sowars were returning, and, after a two-mile's ride, I heard the shouts of the villagers and the cracking of the bushes under the heavy tramp of the cattle. My sowars now showed a very bold front, but there was little need for their help, for, when the Ooblana men saw me riding with the thanadar at my heels, they ran off towards their stronghold, and we drove the buffaloes off towards my boundary.

On reaching the Dachour thana we counted our cattle, and found we had seventy-nine head of fine buffaloes. Those which were fairly proved to belong to Asynduh were restored to their owners, and the thieves were made over eventually to Mr. Clerk for punishment. I got back to Kurnal after a forty-mile's ride, well pleased with my day's work. When I twitted the sowars upon being outdone by a set of cow-drivers, they declared that they were not attacked according to the rules of warfare, but that their opponents got amongst them and set up a screech, on which every buffalo cocked its tail and ran off like mad to the jungles. The vakeel, when he next came to make his *salaam*, execrated his bad luck and his pony, which had run, he said, till the saddle-girths burst. "But, sir," he ended, "I have got rid of the beast, and will ride in a palanquin for the rest of my days."

Such, then, are some of the more active scenes of a magistrate's life in India.

We may now turn to examine briefly the machine over which he presides. Residing ordinarily in the chief town of his district, the magistrate and collector of the north-western provinces (to say nothing of his revenue duties) watches over the police and criminal jurisdiction of a tract of country containing, on an average, some 750,000 souls, and extending, to take one district with another, over 2322 square British statute miles.* This district is parcelled out into revenue and police divisions. The revenue divisions, of which there are from five to ten, or thereabouts, in ordinary districts, are each under a tehsildar, and are only noticed here because this officer has, or ought to have, generally the police charge in his division, or tehsildaree, as it is commonly called. Within this tehsildaree, according to its size and population, two or more thanas, or chief police-stations, are embraced. The tehsildar, as deputy-magistrate, has generally the powers of an assistant-magistrate; that is, can inflict small fines and sentence to short terms of imprisonment in cases made over to him by his superior. He cannot, however, legally take up petitions, though such may be made over to him by the magistrate. It is a common and very convenient practice to call upon the deputy-magistrate to give an opinion, in what are vulgarly called Act IV. of '40 cases; in other words, in cases of forcible dispossession or apprehended breach of the peace, owing to disputes about possession of land, houses, &c. &c. A good tehsildar, as deputy to the magistrate, is a most

* The largest district in the north-west provinces, Goruckpoor, contained, by the last published return, 7346 square miles, and a population of 2,376,533 souls. Delhi and Benares have a comparatively small area, on account of the large cities in those districts, which alone give ample employment to the magistrate.

useful person, and well earns his salary of 200 rupees per mensem; under him comes the police thanadar,* who is, or ought to be, the representative of the tehsildar within the limits of his thana. Volumes have been written about the under-payment of these officers, whose salaries range from twenty-five to fifty rupees per mensem. But, as in a rightly-administered district, the thanadars are to be considered the deputies of the tehsildar in his police capacity, and as they may hope to rise to this higher dignity, it is not so clear, as many persons suppose, that the thanadar of the north-western provinces is altogether underpaid. It is the bounden duty of a district chief, who, as collector as well as magistrate, has much patronage in his gift, to keep his eye on meritorious men; and good thanadars should be made revenue peshkars, or deputy tehsildars, whence the next step is to the tehsildaree. Difficulties, especially with reference to the acquisition of a revenue education by the thanadar, attend the execution of this plan, but they are not insuperable; and, as a general rule, the thanadar should have before him the prospect of one day aspiring to the tehsildaree. His pay then will not be so very much out of proportion to his power, and his condition will be the normal condition of most rising young professional men in Europe, working hard on small emoluments, in the hope of future ad-

* Kotwals get a salary of 100 rupees, or more, in the larger cities.

vancement. True, he has much power; but if his superior, the tehsildar, be held duly responsible for the character of the police in his division, this power will be exercised under an eye well able to detect error, and under a hand well able to repress disorder.

Under the thanadar is the jemadar of police, who acts as his assistant and deputy. There is, too, in each thana, a writer, who has also a deputy; and there are some twenty or thirty burkundaz, the *pedites* of the police force.* Lower still comes the last, but by no means the least important link in the chain of administration, the village watchman or policeman, one of whom is found in each considerable township.

Besides the watchman, there is a nondescript functionary kept in most villages by the landholder, whose duty is to carry information of all important occurrences to the police office, to guide travellers, call the tenants, &c. &c. This *bulahur* or *goreyt* is generally remunerated by a patch of land, granted by the village lords, and his relation to the magistrate is not very clearly defined, either by law or by custom, so far as we know. At the period of the revenue settlement the Government made an abatement in the demand to meet the pay of the watchman; either in money, or by giving up the revenue on their lands. Very high authorities have consi-

* The jemadar and mohurrir get about 8 or 10 rs. per mensem, and the burkundaz gets 4 rs. The village watchman gets seldom more than rs. 2–8 or rs. 2 a month, and certain perquisites (at harvest time) of grain.

dered it desirable that the watchmen should be remunerated for their services by allotments of land, which tend to keep up the feudal relation to the village lords. We, however, conclude on the whole, that the best way to pay the village police is in money, through and by the tehsildar, who should collect the sums due with the revenue, and disburse the same periodically, say every quarter, to the watchmen.

Such, then, is the organisation over which the magistrate of the north-western provinces, aided by his joint magistrate and covenanted assistants, presides. His establishment is generally made more complete by the services of some fifty or more mounted policemen, and on an emergency he can strengthen his police by the temporary aid of his tehsildaree and gaol guards.*

We have already said that the public, as such, give no help to the ministers of justice. But the law has never released the landholders from the responsibility attached from time immemorial to their position, as conservators of the public peace, within the limits of their own estates. On the contrary, many enactments distinctly enforce this condition, and however unwilling or indifferent the village proprietors may be, it must be through their aid and concurrence alone that the police can be

* There are many cases in which it would be absurd for a magistrate to call out the military, yet in which the sight of a few muskets and bayonets would have an excellent effect. The gaol guards, as now organised in most districts, can occasionally thus be used with advantage.

effectual. The magistrate who lets the landed proprietors see, that without needlessly harassing them he will yet never relax his legal demands on their co-operation, and will never pass over their apathy or opposition, takes the surest and shortest road to administrative success. If any supposed advance in legislation loosens this, the chief remaining bond between the magistrate and the people, the consequences upon public peace and order may be serious. As matters now stand, the officers of Government, if they use discreetly but resolutely the powers over the landed proprietors with which the law has armed them, may generally secure the help of the most locally influential classes. For it is clearly the interest as well as the duty of the zemindar to help the police, unless he or his are implicated in a breach of the law. Take an ordinary case of homicide, for instance. A peasant, in a fit of rage or jealousy, cuts down in open day his enemy or his rival. His near relations urge him to fly, but before he has gone far, the village landholders and watchmen, knowing that the magistrate will surely hold them responsible for the open escape of a criminal, raise the hue and cry, and the offender is secured. His arms are tied behind his back, his sword is pulled out of the place where it had been hastily concealed, and off he is marched to the nearest police office, where he generally confesses his guilt, and within four-and-twenty hours he is in the district gaol. More atrocious and secret crimes, such as midnight assassination, or child-murder, for the sake of plunder, are every day detected by the aid and agency of the villagers. The police without this aid can do very little.

When crimes are committed by the landholders themselves, the helplessness of the magistrate without his natural ally the zemindar, is felt plainly enough. Let us consider the case, once so common, of a regular fight with swords and staves—in official language, a case of affray with homicide, in which the rival factions of a village community are engaged. There are two causes which lead to these enormous offences. First, disputed claims to houses, land, trees, fisheries, pastures, or other manorial rights. Secondly, hereditary ill-blood, which causes a predisposition to pugnacity, combined with an innate love of resorting to the sword or club as a clencher to all arguments. The first of these *irritamenta* has been almost taken away by the excellent revenue legislation of late years, which has left no doubt as to boundaries and landed rights in general, and by the working of judicious legislation, which ought to secure the settlement of cases of forcible dispossession in a summary manner. These great improvements leave no excuse for club law; a dispute about property may now be promptly and cheaply disposed of, and cases which, in our own country, would take the parties concerned into Chancery, and keep them there for a lifetime, are daily settled by the magistrates, with the aid of an umpire or a village jury, in the course of a few hours. The moral causes which predispose men, full of pride and vigour, to take the law into their own hands, are not so easily remedied; and many years must pass before we can hope to curb the national defects of temper, or to remedy the popular deficiencies of education. These are shown on every trifling occasion. Let us give an example.

Shere Singh, a violent, proud, and ignorant young Rajpoot, sees a goat trespassing on his sugar-cane or corn-field. Urjun is the owner of the goat, second cousin to Shere Singh, with whom he played as a child, with whom he climbed trees as a boy, and whom as a man he is ready to defend against all the world, out of his own village. But the fathers of these young men live and eat *separately*, the grandfather of one killed the grandfather of the other half-a-century back, and the lands and interests of the two families have long been divided. Shere Singh feels that Urjun's goat has no right in his field; he picks up a clod of earth or a stick, flings it at the animal, which goes limping home with a broken leg. Urjun's father had watched Shere Singh; he comes down from the roof of his house, and abuses the offender at the top of his voice. Urjun comes home, sees the goat which he had bought for his sick child lying helpless on his threshold, sallies out, hears Shere Singh abusing his female relations, and runs to fetch his sword. The villagers gather round; there is a rush, a scuffle, a fight, and, before the sun sets, Urjun and Shere Singh are carried off to the police-office on char-poys in a moribund state, with broken heads and mutilated bodies. Twenty others of the family had been engaged in the *mêlée*, but nobody will tell the police who they were; the wounded scuffle off to the neighbouring villages, the dead or dying are given up to the authorities. Let the village watchman be called, he will give no information, and unless the magistrate succeed in hunting up some stray witness unconnected with the village, the whole affair is left in doubt. So great are the difficulties when the landholder and the police do not pull together.

The regulations for the internal economy of the police force (as detailed in Reg. XX. of 1817) are excellent. The magistrate under these provisions receives daily reports of the distribution of his forces, and of every occurrence which deserves notice. Checks are used to prevent, as far as may be, the falsification or alteration of the written entries made in the books of the country police offices, but no check is so effectual as the eye of a vigilant magistrate. The same men who will *cook* their police reports, and fleece every village in their beat under a feeble or inefficient magistrate, will act with zeal and comparative fidelity when they have to deal with an able master.

This brings us to an important part of our subject,—the treatment of subordinate native official persons by the magistrate. Here, we believe, is one of our most notorious short-comings: English pride and reserve in the treatment of the people of the country have gone far to neutralise English honour and energy. Subjection may be natural to the Indian mind, but it is a subjection mixed with familiarity. "My old master was so kind to me," we once heard a grey-headed chuprassey say, almost with the tears in his eyes,—"such a kind master: "he brought me up, he treated me, *pala*, (*cherished* "*me*), *koota ke mafik* (*like a dog*)." The man's voice faltered; he could praise his old master no farther. Here is the secret of the Indian temperament. Treat the natives with mixed love and severity; if not with the familiarity, yet with the affection shown to dogs, and they will go round the world with you; seek to drive them, as mere horses or beasts of burden, and they will play you a trick the moment your eye is off them. The Oriental vocabularies could supply half-a-dozen synonyms for the word "*murdoom-shinasee*," for which the English language, so far as we remember, has not a single direct equivalent. *Murdoom-shinasee*, literally "the knowledge of men," means the faculty of judging character, of selecting the fittest man for any particular duty. Every one who has read a page of history knows, that of all qualifications for a man in power, this is about the first; yet amongst our mofussil or provincial chiefs, for such we consider magistrates to be, no quality is less thought of or less cultivated. A superficial acquaintance with native character has led many an English officer to conclude that "all (black) men are liars;" and men who are treated as liars will seldom long respect truth. But there are as many and as great variations of character under a dark skin as under a white one, and honesty may be found or may be cultivated as truly, though not so frequently, in the torrid as in the temperate zone. Of all men it most becomes a magistrate to hold free and open intercourse with the people, and then he will soon know the character of his subordinates. Where a native official bears a good repute,—where all men speak of his honesty and fidelity,—there is a dependant who may, within certain bounds and restrictions, be trusted.

Thus may a wise chief note certain grand moral landmarks, thus may he keep within reach certain "*points d'appui*," to which, in time of difficulty, he can look for guidance and support. It is superfluous to add, that a kind, patient, and conciliatory mode of conduct, habitually becomes the man of power in India as in every other country. And nowhere on occasion will the impetuous flash of just indignation work with more instant energy and effect.* The mild, temperate, yet active magistrate, who kindles into fire only on great and pressing occasions, will do far more than one of those stormy characters whose voice is to be ever heard thundering through his cutcherry, or one of those sour spirits who talks to his omlah like a spoiled child to his nurse.

* As an illustration of this part of our subject, we are tempted to give an anecdote related to us by an accomplished civil officer of high rank in the north-west: his informant was Sir E. Colebrooke. Mr. Seton (afterwards resident at Delhi) held some important office (probably that of Governor-general's Agent) in Rohilcund. There was a fermentation among the Puthans at Bareilly, and a meditated insurrection. Seton, sending for the principal Mahometans, called on them to allay the evil feeling. Amongst others came the cazee, a notorious old scoundrel, whom Seton addressed with all the courtesy of a

But if the *suaviter in modo* be desirable, no less necessary is the *fortiter in re*. Orientals are like children, and it is a due firmness and severity, blended with the kinder feelings of the heart, which can alone secure their devotion. Your kind, easy man, who likes to see the people about his bench with fine shawls and sun-shiny faces, who cannot say *No* to the importunities of his omlah, does as much harm to a district as your mofussil Nero, who speaks habitually to men of rank in the accents of a whipper-in rating a hound.

In short, whether a magistrate is too proud and distant, or too easy and yielding, the result is the same. In the first case, he will not hear the people's voice; in the second case, he will hear it only through certain official mouth-pieces, whose object will be to deceive and to cajole him. In either case, the darling sin of Eastern satraps will have full scope: malversation will spread across the length and breadth of the country.

Whilst touching on the subject of malversation, we may venture a few remarks on the peculiar reasons which make the personal character and

gentleman of the old school. The cazee made difficulties and objections. Seton was convinced that this man was at the bottom of all the mischief brewing, but went on mildly admonishing him, to no effect; when, firing up, he seized the cazee by the beard, and shaking his (the cazee's) head backwards and forwards, exclaimed, "Suno Cazee Jee, hum nurum ho sukta aur "hum gurum ho sukta." ("Listen, Mister Cazee,—I can be "gentle, but I can be rough too.")

The cazee was frightened to death, gave in at once, went home to the citizens, and stopped all the agitation.

disposition of the magistrate so important in India. The honour of our country is associated with his name. By the people at large he is looked up to, not as a mere functionary, however powerful, but as the State, the Sirkar, the personification of British Government. However pure and upright his conduct (and such we believe the conduct of our magistrates in general to be), however benevolent his intentions, yet the people will consider him neither pure nor good, if his native subordinates are allowed, unchecked, to practise corruption and extortion. A proud, idle, or soft magistrate, will fail to exercise a pure administration, however honourable his private character may be.

History at large is the hand-book of statesmen, but if there be one page of it more worthy the study of an Indian officer than another, it is the history of malversation. For though the arts of corruption are as old as the civilisation of man, though they luxuriate as freely in the snows of Russia as in the sands of Asia, India has ever been their chosen home. But India may none the less take a lesson from Europe. Above all there is one period, and a very interesting one it is, in the history of Rome, which seems to us full of instruction to the rulers of British India: we allude to the century and a half which preceded the establishment of the Imperial power under Julius Cæsar. No men ever suffered more from the curse of misgovernment than did the provincial subjects of Rome during this period. The sons of Rome left every Roman virtue behind them, and adopted every foreign vice, when once they passed the frontiers of their parent soil. The proconsuls of the Republic,—men of talent, of good birth, of tried experience,—on reaching their distant provinces, devoted every energy to the bad art of turning civil power into gold. Rome execrated her corrupt sons, but she failed, distant and distracted as she was, to restrain their corruption. And so the Roman provincials went on suffering, as men never suffered before, whilst their women, their gold, their painted vestments, were torn from them to encumber the proconsular trains. It mattered little to the subject wretches of Greece, of Syria, or of Sicily, that Roman law was strict, that Roman virtue was proverbial. They saw Rome only in the shape of a tyrant who debauched their women, and plundered their treasuries: the will of the proconsul was their law, his lusts their doom. Now to apply this to our subject.

We live in no ordinary times. The splendour which seemed to surround Rome, when first she bore the sceptre of the world, gathers fast round our Eastern empire. Let Englishmen beware, lest, dazzled by the brilliancy of their position, they lose sight of the necessities of the people. Let them take warning from Rome. As it was with Italy, so it is with England. Her sons, speaking a strange tongue, administering strange laws, enforcing them by still stranger powers, pushing on alike the arts of war and peace, dictate supremely, as did the Romans of old, to millions of subjects, differing alike from themselves and from one another. England has her own cares, her own distractions, as Rome had before her. Her political sympathies with India are no stronger than those of Rome were with Macedonia; her social sympathies are infinitely less than those of Rome were with Greece. England has only a few chosen men, who devote themselves with an intelligent zeal to the strengthening her Eastern empire; their influence, if considerable, is still remote. All then, or nearly all, depends on the local Government, whose type is to be found not only in the palaces of Calcutta or Agra, but also in the cutcherries of those representatives of Government who, as commissioners, judges, magistrates, or collectors of revenue, preside over the immediate destinies of India. All that the Roman proconsul was, or might have been, to the provincials of Rome, these officers are to the people of India. The Indian Governments must be judged, not only by the ability and zeal of governors and secretaries, but by the character of the men who carry on the every-day executive functions of the state. Happily for us and for India, the rule with these our proconsuls is what was the exception with the Roman deputies: we can point to many whose hearts are devoted to the happiness of the people, —not to one whose energies are given to their ruin. Such a man, indeed, a modern Verres or Dolabella, belonging to our own patrician order, could not hope to hide his vices for a single day from a Government ever jealous of English honour.

All this is well. We bestow more affection on the people than Rome ever spared to her distant provincials, whilst we have not to thank our subjects, as Rome had to thank hers, for either science or taste, for marbles instinct with life, or for the kindred arts of poetry and painting. We repeat, this is so far good and generous.

None the less it may be asked, Is England fulfilling all the duties which India requires at her hands? Are the men of England in India doing all that as Englishmen—above all, as Christians—may be demanded of them? Boasting of their moral strength, are they not still weak, in that they too lightly consider the moral weakness of the people?

It is not enough to answer to these questions that the English servants of Government are honest, pure, high-minded men. The question remains, Are they jealous of the purity and honesty of others who exercise power in their name and on their behalf?

Here, we believe, is the weakest point in the English administration of India. Men, pure and high-minded themselves, yield to a *supposed* necessity of impurity and corruption in others. To sell justice may long have been common amongst the natives of Hindostan, yet surely that judge is not blameless who presides in a court where many, at least, of the minor processes of justice are commonly bought and sold. Corruption may not be open; no man cries stinking fish: but that must not satisfy a jealous guardian of the law. It is his *duty*, however painful, to suspect, to hunt out, and on due occasion to denounce, dishonest acts; it belongs to him to sweep away these old superstitions about custom and necessity, not to bury his head in them as an ostrich buries her head in the sand. Above all, his very first and most special duty is to teach the people that injustice, however customary, is never necessary, and that honesty, however rare amongst the native officials, is the best policy all the world over. And for this we must look to our district officers, and not to the Supreme Government alone.

But here the insular pride and good nature of English judges equally interpose between them and justice. The high-minded Englishman cannot make up his mind to listen to the tale of informers; he cannot bring himself to pry into suspicious papers and accounts; nor will the kind, easy master, on the other hand, believe that his well-dressed, bland *omlah*, are a set of rapacious villains. All this suspicion and smelling out of crime, he argues, is fitter for a Bow Street officer than for a gentleman: so it may be; yet if the English gentleman chooses to sit in an Indian cutcherry, he is bound to think of the people as well as of his own tastes and habits. He must learn to sacrifice, or at all events to mortify, the feelings with which he has been brought up, whether of pride or of softness. If he argues that it is beneath him to pry into the dirty intrigues of native officials, he is wrong, for it is never beneath an Englishman to do his duty.

The circumstances of the country demand of the judge that he should be not the judge only, but the advocate of the people. Even Rome could on occasion produce her orators to denounce, in never-dying words, the atrocities of provincial corruption. We need not repeat, that corruption is not the weakness of English gentlemen of the present day; but it is, and long will be, the darling sin of their Indian subordinate officers. And thus the English sin by deputy. They do not encourage corruption, but neither do they extinguish it. They make up their minds that an evil is necessary, when they ought only to determine that the necessity exists no longer. The whole question is an unpleasant and disagreeable one, so it is pushed out of sight.

But the people of India, whose wits are as keen to detect official iniquity as, unhappily, they are prone to practise it, are not thus to be satisfied. They love to see an extortioner or oppressor brought low, and they consider him, and him only, an upright judge who looks for uprightness in his subordinates. It is, then, clearly the duty of our countrymen to put down with a strong hand the malversation of native officials. How often (to compare small rogues to great ones) have these Indian satraps been to their jurisdiction what Verres was to Sicily, what Dolabella was to Macedonia. Men of this stamp should be hunted out and denounced, without scruple or compunction. What the youthful Cæsar was to Dolabella, what Cicero was to Verres, this must the English magistrate be to any rapacious subordinate. Solicitude for the people may well supply to the Christian judge that righteous zeal which ambition or policy furnished to the heathen advocate.

The fate of one corrupt official, whose villanies

have been fairly brought home to him, and have met with worthy punishment, will be a lesson to entire provinces, and will deter hundreds from a career of extortion and plunder.

We are glad to believe that in this respect matters are mending. Corrupt men and corrupt *omlah* still are to be found, but they form the exception, not the rule, and their number is, we trust, decreasing. A fixed plan of promotion, depending not on seniority but on merit, will do wonders for them as it has done for their European superiors. In the judicial department, it is remarkable that a native judge, who has any prospect of promotion, hardly ever is known to be corrupt. Sudder ameens at the top of the tree, who can rise no higher, and obscure moonsiffs whose lack of ability leaves them no hope of promotion, are the only men who are now suspected of taking bribes. Amongst the police, corrupt thanadars are still too common, but dishonest tehsildars and deputy-magistrates are few and far between.

The revenue training which most of our district officers have undergone, by throwing them into constant unreserved habits of intercourse with the people, has had an immense though indirect effect upon the criminal and police administration of the upper provinces. Men in power have learned the inestimable advantages of being accessible, at all due times and places, to the people. They have learned, too, that ignorance about their people and districts is not a necessary evil, but a crime. When men knew not what the resources of the country were, knew neither the geography nor the statistics of their districts, it was not to be supposed that they would study very exactly the habits, manners, or feelings of the several tribes therein. But it were a shame for a magistrate, with all the varied information which his revenue office *now* affords him, to remain in the dark as to any important fact or distinction bearing on the welfare of the people. The best rule he can lay down for himself is, to carry into his cutcherry, as magistrate, the same feelings and habits which he has learned as a collector or settlement officer. A reserved, haughty, distant, inaccessible revenue officer, is of about as much real use as a blind miniature painter or a deaf musician. His very element is, or ought to be, popularity; and it is not much otherwise with a magistrate. Let him, when out of doors, forbid access to no man: he will find it a good rule to listen to *all* who interrupt his walk or his ride: if the suitor complain against his neighbour, let him be referred at once to the open cutcherry, as the proper arena for disputes between man and man: if he complain of the officers of Government subordinate to the magistrate, let the complainant have due encouragement to open out his grievance. This will cut short petty tyranny and extortion.

It is quite possible for a magistrate to go regularly to his court,* yet still to give no fair audience

* We do not allude to the case, now, we believe, a very rare one, of magistrates who neglect their bounden duty of daily going to cutcherry when at their station. Such men we have known in by-gone days, who would say, "There is nothing to

to his people. Once a-day they should, at a stated time, be invited to bring their petitions openly to the head of the district, and to say out what they have to say, without fear of any man. They will soon find that it is of no use bringing trumpery complaints against one another or against the police officers, but that no real abuse will be allowed to pass without inquiry.

Having ventured to lay down these rules for a magistrate, we will conclude this part of our subject by assuring district officers that a firm, yet mild and generous, treatment of their numerous subordinates, will be accepted with gratitude by none more than the subordinates themselves. A discriminating eye, as well as a kind hand, is what every native who is fit for the public service highly appreciates; and, as a body, our police officers will be grateful and attached to a good magistrate. If only he will treat them as Claudian tells us Theodosius treated his soldiers, he will meet a like reward.

> " Pœnæ parcus erat, . . . . . . . .
> . . . . . . . . largitor honorum;
> Pronus, et in melius gaudens convertere fata;
> Hinc amor, hinc validum, devoto milite, robur."

Before leaving this part of our subject we give

do in my district." There is a very short way to arrive at this state of things: all magistrates have only to do nothing, and the people will soon enable them to say with truth, that "there is nothing to do."—"*Solitudinem faciunt et pacem appellant.*"

This mischievous class of public men is nearly extinct, and they do perhaps less harm in the north-western provinces than in other parts of India; for here the people, if they cannot get justice, will soon take the law into their own hands.

an instance of the harm which a single hasty order by the magistrate may cause, in the following extract from our friend's "Note-Book."

### Beerbul the Bhoorjee.

I have never been able to make up my mind whether it is right and proper for the head of a district to make over a part of his police reports to a joint or assistant-magistrate for orders: if he do not give the younger officers in the service some separate police charge they will have little opportunity for learning how to manage a district, and will take less interest in their duties than when they are entrusted with a distinct responsibility. On the other hand, such evils arise from a slight apparent error, from a seemingly trifling inconsideration, that one trembles to place the powerful lever of police authority in the hands of an inexperienced workman. An incautious nod of the head in the cutcherry may cause the ruin of whole families in the mofussil. A careless dissent to the proposition of a subordinate may involve an entire village in riot and bloodshed. Here is an instance of the evil resulting from an inconsiderate though well-intentioned order.

I was, in 184—, walking through the ward of my gaol in which prisoners under trial were kept. Here were assembled, not only men committed by me to take their trial at the sessions-court, but also the prisoners from a neighbouring district, whose cases were pending before the same tribunal. Men awaiting their trial generally have a good deal to say, to very little purpose, to the magistrate, when he comes to inspect their ward. Amongst others who addressed me was a middle-aged man, with small, red-looking, wild eyes, grizzled hair, and a peculiar forehead, which ran back into a point, so that one could fancy it moulded in the form of an equilateral triangle, with the eyebrows for the base line. The manner of this prisoner was as singular as his appearance, whilst he kept reiterating, "They killed my child! they killed my child! I brought him up from so high," stooping down and holding the flat of his hand a few inches from the ground: "I watched him and cherished him, but they killed him, without any fault or crime." On inquiry, the gaol darogah informed me that the prisoner was on his trial for murder, committed in the neighbouring district, and that the child which he kept lamenting was a pet tree, which had been cut down by the police. My curiosity was so far excited, that when a native visitor a few days later asked me whether I had heard of the murder which had been perpetrated in the —— district, owing to the cutting down of a tree, I at once begged to hear the particulars. My informant had, I suspect, been on an unsuccessful expedition to the said district in quest of employment, which may account for a certain degree of bitterness pervading his narrative, but the facts related by him are, as I have reason to know, not far from the truth.

"Beerbul, who is now in your honour's gaol,

and about to take his trial for murder before the sessions-judge, is a bhoorjee, or parcher of grain, by profession. He was always considered a quiet, decent man. Next door to him lived a Marwarrie money-lender, named Putnee Mul, a bunyan by trade, but with a heart like a butcher, and so famous for avarice, that if by mishap any man took his name in the morning on an empty stomach, he would get no dinner that day unless he beat his shoes five times on the ground, crying, 'God forgive me!' each time. Putnee Mul grudged to spend an anna, even in the funeral ceremonies of his own father, but could always find a few rupees to bribe the police to worry his neighbours. Well, as I said, he lived next door to the bhoorjee, and, as a matter of course, they hated each other. The bhoorjee had no children; he was an odd reserved sort of man, and cared for nobody except his old wife, and for nothing except one pet tree, which he had planted when a boy, and married, after his own marriage, to a well in his court-yard. Every morning he and his wife, after their daily ablutions, poured water over the tree; which, in short, they looked upon as their child. As bad luck would have it, a branch of this tree grew gradually over a part of the Marwarrie money-lender's roof. When the water dropped from this branch in the rainy season it washed away a small portion of the mud plaster, and the repairs cost Putnee Mul two pice. This was ruinous; so he went to the bhoorjee, and told him to cut the offending branch of his tree off.

The bhoorjee got angry at the idea of mutilating his beloved tree, and gave Putnee Mul a cross answer.

"Off went the money-dealer to the thanadar, and, putting five rupees into his hand, begged him to report to the magistrate that the bhoorjee's tree opened a road for thieves to his house, and ought to be cut down. The report went before the junt sahib (joint-magistrate, whose experience, be it said with respect, is limited), and the order came for cutting down the tree. Two burkundazes were sent to the village, who laid hold of a couple of labourers, and cut down the tree, whilst Putnee Mul looked on with a satisfied grin from the roof of his house. In the evening the bhoorjee came home, with a basket of leaves for his oven on his head, found his wife crying and beating her breast, and his doorway blocked up with the fallen tree. Putnee Mul called out to him, 'Well, Beerbul, will you do as I bid you in future, or not?' Beerbul was silent; but murder was in his heart.

"Next morning, as Putnee Mul came out in the early dawn with his *lotah* in his hand, he saw what looked like three lights under the wall of the bhoorjee's house; two of these were the blood-red eyes of the bhoorjee, the third was his match. The next moment the Marwarrie was on the ground, with four bullets from Beerbul's match-lock in his heart.

"With a yell of triumph the bhoorjee sprung on his prey, and, ere yet the death-struggles were over, drew his rusty sword, and hacking off the arms and then the head of his victim, stuck them on the mutilated trunk and branches of his darling tree. He then bent down over the dead body and drank, out of the hollow of his hand, three mouthfuls of his enemy's blood. This done, he reloaded his matchlock, and, armed with it, with sword, dagger, and bow and arrows, took his post on the roof of his house. 'Now,' he cried, 'let 'the thanadar come who dared to rob me of my 'child, my only child, and I'll serve him as I 'served this cursed Marwarrie.'

"Hours passed on, but none were found bold enough to seize the bhoorjee, whose matchlock was pointed at any human being who came near. Towards evening a dog came to smell at the body of the Marwarrie, but Beerbul pinned him to the ground with an arrow.

"The police surrounded the place, and the thanadar had a charpoy put for him under a tree beyond the range of Beerbul's matchlock. All Putnee Mul's money-bags would not have tempted him within the bhoorjee's reach. So passed the day, and so the night. Next day the voice of the woman could be heard encouraging her husband, as she handed him up a pitcher of water and a cake of bread: 'Well done, rajah! die like a man, 'and *never* let them tie your hands.' Well, sir, to make a long story short, the bhoorjee was caught at last, but not by fair means.

"When the news of his resistance reached the sudder station, various expedients for taking him alive were discussed. Everybody had a plan, but nobody's plan was approved. At last a little Mahometan writer, named Jan Ali, belonging to the collector's office, stepped forward and said, 'If the junt magistrate sahib will order his slave to go to the aid of the police, the bhoorjee shall, by the good fortune of the Kumpanee Buhadoor, be captured.' The junt sahib assented, and the bystanders applauded Jan Ali for his devotion. 'Here is my sword,' said one; 'here is my pony,' said another. 'I want no sword,' said Jan Ali; 'but give me that old book of medicine belonging 'to the dufturee: I want nothing else.'

"'He is going to work some sort of spell,' said the bystanders: 'well, contrivance is better 'than force, especially when one has to do with 'such a *kafir* as this bhoorjee.' Such were the criticisms passing round as Jan Ali set off, with his thin legs sticking far out of his broad white trowsers, whilst he kicked his heels into the nazir's pony, one hand on the mane, the other clasping the medicine-book.

"When he arrived at the scene of Putnee Mul's murder the shades of evening were closing in. The bhoorjee had been two days and a night watching his enemy's corpse, and began to get rather tired. A villager was sent to scream out to him that a message had come from the magistrate. The bhoorjee put down his matchlock and invited the messenger to a parley. Jan Ali came, book in hand, and saluting Beerbul, informed him that the magistrate, admiring his courage, had offered a pardon, if he would come quietly down from the roof of his house. (This, I need not inform you, sir, was a devise of Jan Ali's, and not any order of the magistrate's.) 'Who are 'you?' said Beerbul. 'They call me Syed Jan 'Ali,' was the reply, 'and I am the chief Kazi 'of ——.' 'A Syed, are you?' replied Beerbul; 'will you swear that my hands shall not be tied 'if I come down?' 'On the Koran,' said Jan Ali, producing the medicine-book, and reverently holding it out on the palms of his hands, with his eyes turned up to heaven. The bhoorjee came down, when four burkundazes pounced upon him, kicked him, and, tying his arms with a strong rope, led him away like a wild beast. 'Oh!' said he, 'Kazi jee, I thought my arms were not to be 'tied.' Jan Ali replied, with a smile, 'That is 'the way we catch murderers;' and so the bhoorjee was carried off, the policemen looking very big with drawn swords and lighted matches all round him."

Here ended my informant's story.

I watched the progress of Beerbul's case with interest. The civil surgeon of —— pronounced him mad, and another medical man, on seeing him and hearing his history, hinted that all was accounted for by the shape of his head, "for in the "whole course of his life he had never seen such "a developement of the organ of firmness." It was, however, proved, that the man had never been mad, nor suspected of madness, till he killed the Marwarrie, and was then, and at the time of trial, quite capable of distinguishing between right and wrong; so it ended in Beerbul's being sent to the *kala panee*, or black water, as transportation is termed up the country. Now here, owing to a single inconsiderate, though by no means ill-intended order, one man lost his life, another his liberty, and two families were plunged into ruin and misery.

NOTE.—Writing from camp, we defer the examination of comparative criminal statistics promised in page 186 of this volume, and the continuation of the "Memorandum on the Rise and Progress of Criminal Law in the Bengal Presidency," till our return to the comforts of a library.

# VIII.

## NOTES ON THE POLICE.

---

We have attempted already to sketch the relative positions of an English magistrate in Upper India and the body of the people, and it remains only to consider him *en rapport* to the Government.

There is much to tempt men in power in India, and above all, magistrates; to fancy themselves omnipotent, and to lead them to exclaim with the French monarch, "*L'état, c'est moi.*" But an Indian magistrate by no means escapes the conditions of modern power, and with many slaves he has, too, no short allowance of masters.

And here we come to a constitutional defect, if not an organic disorder, in our system of government; for, whilst the magistrate owns allegiance to a whole host of authorities, not any one of these authorities is in the position effectually either to support or to control him.

The Government may smash the Magistrate, the Nizamut Adawlut or the Commissioner of Police may snub him, the Sessions Judge may worry him, Inspectors of Prisons or of Road Police may trouble and perplex him, but not one of these superiors is able fully to test his merits or to remedy his failings.

The evil of this systematic defect may not be felt when, as at present, the government is conducted by a statesman who is closely acquainted with the merits of his subordinate officers. But, when another Pharaoh comes who knows not Joseph, when the magistrates are left to prove their worth, if they can, merely through the regular channels of official routine, they will have little beyond their own sense of duty to guide or encourage them in labours as arduous as often fall to the lot of man. For, to consider *seriatim* the *custodes* of the *custodes* of Upper India,—

First, we have his honour the Lieutenant-governor of the North-western Provinces.

Now, we repeat, so long as we have in this noble office a man who studies the official character of all the more prominent officers under him as a pilot studies his ground, not only by chart, but, so to speak, by actual soundings,—so long as the foremost man in the ranks of the up-country service be chosen to rule at Agra, no good magistrate will be overlooked. But, for all that, the exertions of able magistrates may fail to attract the same attention as the performances of efficient revenue officers. The cause of this is not justly to be traced to any indifference on the part of the Government as to how the people of the country are treated, so long as the Government share of the resources of the country are duly realised. No, it is to a very different reason that we must attribute the insufficient hold which the Government of India has on the magistrate. English law has, perhaps, more to do with the matter than Oriental rapacity. But this we can better show when we come to consider the magistrate's second master, namely, the Sudder Nizamut Adawlut, or Supreme Court of Criminal Judicature, which stands next in rank to the head of the State. Before this tribunal the record of all the judicial acts of the magistrate, duly registered monthly, passes. The Sudder judges also constantly have his proceedings in criminal cases under review. But, in India as in England, the judges hold no administrative responsibility to the Government. They are supreme and unfettered, and do not consider it within the limit of their ordinary jurisdiction to weigh nicely the merits of each magistrate, or the nature of his work. The acts of the Government itself, as every one knows, are liable to be called in question before their tribunals, and virtually the judges are independent of the administrator of the State. Under these circumstances, which, be it observed, result from an imitation of the constitutional law of England, it were absurd to expect from a judge of the Sudder Nizamut Adawlut a reasonable opinion as to the merits or efficiency of any particular magistrate. Ask such a judge what is the public character of any one of the district magistrates, and he will candidly confess that he is unable to give a decided opinion.*

But the qualifications of the same man as a revenue officer are subjected to a far more close and immediate scrutiny by the Board of Revenue, which is directly subordinate to the local Government, and responsible for the control of the Collectors of Revenue. It not only belongs to this Board to test accurately the qualifications of all their subordinates, but also to keep the Government informed of their estimate of each and all.

We do not complain of the independence of the judicial officers, but merely offer this explanation of the causes which tend to exalt the office of Collector over that of Magistrate. The Collector being more immediately and closely watched by one powerful department, has a better opportunity of proving his abilities than the magistrate whose entire official career comes under no such immediate scrutiny. For all the judicial acts of the magistrate come under the review of the Sessions Judge or the Supreme Criminal Court only, and these judges having no authority over the magistrate in police matters, are not in the position to form an accurate estimate of his calibre.

Let us go on now to consider the Commissioner of Police, who comes third amongst the superiors of our magistrates. This high official, who is, or ought

* We allude here to the Sudder Judges at Agra. In the Calcutta court, we have reason to believe, that a closer watch is kept over the criminal proceedings in the lower courts.

to be, responsible directly to the Government for the police in his division,* has, on the whole, the best opportunity of appreciating the labours of the magistrate. But he has no power either to control or to support the judicial acts of a district chief.

In fact, he can only see the magistrate's conduct officially from one point, and can test his efficiency simply as an administrator of police, not as a judge in criminal cases. For all this, if the Commissioner habitually and systematically gives as much of his time and attention to the police, as to the revenue concerns of his division, he may be an instrument of extensive good to the people. It belongs to him not only to exhort, encourage, or, if need be, rebuke the magistrates; but he should closely scrutinise, by local inquiry, the character of every native police authority in his jurisdiction. He should know, minutely, the peculiar strong or weak points in the administration of each district, and carry a good magistrate over every obstacle. The intimate acquaintance which, as the "eye of the Government," he ought to have with the state of public feeling in each part of his division, will enable him to form a correct estimate of the relative value of the district officers. As for the mere figured monthly reports of crime, these alone will show little. One of the first results of efficient district management, following upon laxity, may be an apparent increase of

* The Revenue Commissioners are also superintendents of police in the upper provinces, and we hope ere long to see them invested with similar powers in Bengal.

crime. The proportion between crime and punishment may be a surer test, but even this cannot always be implicitly trusted. One of the most unfailing of all possible criteria of a magistrate's character is the "*vox populi*," which in India, as in other places, can hardly be mistaken in a matter where popular interests are so deeply concerned. But whilst we advocate the most anxious supervision, and recommend the police commissioner ever to keep a ready ear and open eye; we as distinctly deprecate anything like a needless spirit of meddlesome interference. If we may borrow a metaphor from naval life, we would dub our commissioners as "quarter-masters," whose part it is to guide carefully the vessel of the State so far as their own watch extends. It is their business to keep a sharp eye on the ship's head and compass, and to warn the helmsman of any error in his course; not to knock him on one side, to seize hold of the helm, or let the halyards fly.

In matters of police the Commissioner corresponds directly with the Government. Now, though praise will do more good to a deserving officer than any other stimulant, we protest against its indiscriminate use, until it degenerates into the "butter" of vulgar life. The annual police reports of some of our commissioners present rather too much of this smooth and unctuous lubricity, and remind us of the confabulation between the Sudder Judge and the Registrar in the olden time:—

*Sudder Judge.*—"Is the annual report ready?"

*Registrar.*—"Quite ready."

*Sudder Judge.*—"Have you praised all the judges?"

*Registrar.*—"All."

*Sudder Judge.*—"Then send it off."

The upshot then, so far as the police is concerned, is just this—the Commissioner may, if he pleases, do very much for the country. He ought to be the eye of the Government; but it depends on the man whether the office be a great or as mall one. It is as he may please to make it, the proconsulship of a wide province, or a species of post-office *ambulante*.

The fourth superior under whom the magistrate labours is the Sessions Judge. This officer has power to do nothing in a district, but to undo everything, if he pleases. Happily for the magistrates and for the people, Indian judges act generally with generosity as well as judgment, and use their powers discreetly. But for this, so great is the encouragement to appeal upon appeal which the law gives, the magistrates would be unable to maintain public order. When a judge ascends the bench, who, from some defect of mind or temperament, is incapable of taking up cases, except with the pettifogging animus of a small English attorney, the result upon the police of a district is most mischievous. For it is needless to say, that in a state of society such as exists in India, men should be encouraged to the utmost to love equity, truth, and good faith, above all things. What can it do but harm to the Indian *morale* to see an English judge exalting the letter of the law above its spirit? A quibbling, hairsplitting judge, who instinctively prefers the legal to the equitable aspect of a question, is a public misfortune. Such a man, throwing away the very arms with which his education, as an Englishman, might have furnished him, descends into the arena to combat crime and intrigue with weapons at which every little Indian lawyer is his master. At the same time, it behoves the magistrate to beware lest by any fault of his excuse be given for an over-zealous regard to the mere letter of the law on the part of the judge; for if the executive authority be tempted to issue an illegal order, or to do an arbitrary act, who shall blame the superior court for setting things right? It may be a weakness to cling too fondly to the law, but it is a sin knowingly to neglect it. So, once for all, we urge upon the notice of the magistracy old John Selden's rule, "Eat within your stomach, act within your commission."*

Pass we on now to number five of the magistrate's masters.

The Inspector of Prisons claims a share of his allegiance. District officers complain, but we think without sufficient reason, of the increased trouble thrown upon them by the inspector's demand for

* Seek, above all things, we would urge upon every young civil officer,—seek, above all things, to obtain a *sound judicial animus*, and to acquire the principles of English law, as bearing upon the weight of evidence and other cognate points. A legal education, strictly so called, may not be within your reach, but judicial training is open to your choice, and every opportunity should be seized of giving a judicial tone and temper to your proceedings.

sundry returns and prison statistics. It cannot be denied that the labours of the gaol establishments have been increased since the appointment of an inspector, but the health and safe custody of the prisoners have been secured in proportion. Indeed, if we were asked to point out a modern measure combining in a remarkable degree economy, humanity, and progress, it is this appointment of a general inspectorship of prisons we should name.* The services of an able and intelligent officer have been secured for the sole object of reforming prison discipline, and a mass of statistical information has been acquired which cannot fail to supply the material for progressive improvement in this important, but once neglected department. Already an advance is apparent in the condition of the convict population, who are gradually being protected from extra-judicial punishment in the shape of disease caused by filth or crowding, and, at the same time, are subjected to a more strict and equal penal discipline. But, to revert to our subject, the magistrate's labour and anxiety are not lessened, and a fifth superior is added to the list.

Number six, in districts through which the Grand Trunk Road passes, is the Superintendant of Police and Inspector of Halting-grounds thereon.†

* Let us hope to see a similar appointment made in Bengal, where it is much wanted.

† Road and canal officers, in some districts, add much to the cares of the magistrate, who has to keep matters smooth if he can, and to prevent the people from growing restive under the inconveniences which the progress of public works causes.

It is the last straw which breaks the camel's back, and if, under these many masters, a magistrate, who, as collector of revenue, has also to obey a long list of fiscal authorities, sometimes gets bewildered or out of patience, it is no great wonder. Nay, the wonder rather is that, on the whole, the volumes of official correspondence contain so slight a tinge of bitterness, and that so much good feeling pervades the relations of official life.

If our reflections are just, if the magistrates have too many masters and too little direct responsibility, it may be worth considering whether some remedy to this defect in our criminal administration can be devised. Our own persuasion is, that such a remedy might be found very near at hand, merely by demanding from the commissioners of police a more close account of their stewardship, and a more intelligent estimate of the state of local police in their several districts. They should be directed to send for a certain number of cases decided by the magistrate, and report specifically on his judicial as well as police capacity. Such reports, embracing the whole field of administrative performance, should be called for at least twice a-year.*

* As it is, some commissioners of revenue, who are versed not only in every rule of their craft, but also in every shade of official aptitude displayed by their subordinate collectors, assume too often in police matters the habit of those old Italian friars, who dubbed themselves *Fratres Ignorantiæ*, and answered all questions with their one word, *Nescio*. Or, if they are not honest enough to avow their ignorance of the minutiæ of

To return to our police magistrate. He has, let us suppose, by combining tact with energy, succeeded in satisfying his official superiors and in keeping the people of his district in good temper and order. There remains another and a very important task. He must secure, if possible, the comfort and safety of the innumerable travellers, who for many hours of each day and night swarm along the high roads of his district.

Thanks to the incessant attention of the local government in the north-west, this part of district duty is much simplified. Every magistrate has abundant instructions at hand, and every facility is given to him by his superiors to complete a chain of arrangements, embracing the convenience of travellers of all ranks. And as yet the system of the up-country shines by contrast with the "*laissez aller*" fashions of the lower provinces.

No sooner does the traveller from Bengal or Behar cross the stream, whose ill-omened waters *

police administration, as affecting the various classes of society in their divisions, there is none the less an indistinct, hazy atmosphere, hanging over their annual police reports, through which the ruling powers can hardly be expected clearly to see their way. Nothing like gross inefficiency or decided disorder would escape observation, but the relative degrees of excellence in district work are passed over in a manner disheartening to the ablest and most laborious amongst the public servants.

* The Hindoos consider it a defilement to touch the waters of the Caramnasa river.

divide these provinces from our north-western territory, than he observes signs of comfort and security to which as yet he has been a stranger. Instead of an occasional dog-kennel-looking hut, or (as in Ramgurh) an elevated bird-watcher's platform, tenanted by a half-starved village-watchman, the wanderer begins to see strong police-stations every two or three miles along the road, with stout, well-armed patrols of horse and foot. Serais, with open gates, invite the weary traveller, whilst, at convenient distances, encamping-grounds are marked out, and supplies for man and beast stored in commodious buildings.

*Apropos* to the matter of supplies, we must digress for a few moments to give due credit to the authorities for the pains which they have taken in arrangements, which, to the mere English reader, may seem so far from—perhaps, so far beneath—the notice of the Government. The disciple of Adam Smith may be inclined to remind us that in a populous and productive country, such as Upper India generally is, supply and demand will, under a good rule, regulate themselves, and that any interference on the part of the Government must be not only superfluous, but mischievous. And so, no doubt, it would be, if the line of march lay betwixt London and Coventry, instead of between Delhi and Benares. But in India such reasoning will not hold good, for so great is the dread in the national mind, and, doubtless, so well founded, of men armed either with authority or with more material arms, that the supply will not answer to the demand in their case.

Under our Mahometan predecessors the march of an army caused at least as much misery as the utmost terrors of war cause in European countries. Nay, even in days of peace the mere progress of an emperor was marked by desolation, pestilence, and famine, and might be tracked by blasted harvests and smoking villages. Nor, as the English flag surmounted one by one the imperial strongholds, were matters in this respect at once and entirely altered for the better. No exertions of the British could restrain their soldiers and followers from the work of plunder and destruction. Even in later days, and in spite of the most stringent orders, the march of troops came like a fall of locusts on our provinces; and, owing to the increasing general tranquillity and civilisation of the country, these visitations year after year were more severely felt. This was not the fault of the military authorities alone, for hungry men with arms in their hands, who find the ordinary markets closed against them, will naturally enough help themselves. As yet the civil powers had established no sufficient system for securing at once the comfort of the troops and the protection of the country people. When an army or a regiment was expected, hurried orders were sent to the district officers to prepare supplies, but how those supplies were to be got together nobody cared. The consequence was, that some tehsildar, or police-officer, laid the country round under contribution, whereby he hoped to supply the troops with forage. Sheep, fowls, cattle were hunted out and carried off to the encampment, the merchant was deprived of his cart, the ploughman of his bullocks, artisans and labourers were dragged from their homes, and a scene of injustice and extortion took place, which the people did not forget for months after. To save their own credit, the native civil-officers had to pay a *douceur* to the head men of the military bazaar, which they (the civil subordinates) in their turn levied from the landholders in the neighbourhood. The natural result of all this was the desertion of villages along the line of march, and especially near the usual places of encampment. Such a state of disorder could not last long after the completion of those reforms in the management of the land revenue which we have on former occasions described; and during the last few years especially the Government has taken a deep interest in the matter, and a regular system for the supply of provisions to all large bodies of travellers has been matured and carried into execution.

Encamping grounds at regulated distances have been marked off.* Contractors for all sorts of necessary supplies have been encouraged by advances of money to settle, and have been furnished with convenient storehouses and shelter. Regular tables of price-current have been prepared in the English and vernacular languages, duly countersigned; the weights and measures have all been

* Shady spots have been selected, or, if such could not be obtained, young trees have been planted.

tested and approved; even the very flour-sieves have been stamped with the official seal. All these details may seem trifling, but the effect of attention to such trifles on the comfort of the troops, and on the happiness of the people, is immense. A regiment marches into a town now without causing any greater excitement than the arrival of a pleasure train from London causes to the good people of Brighton or Epsom. Decent civil officials, under the orders of an assistant or deputy-magistrate, supplied with full credentials, and with instructions how to act in every sort of emergency, attend alike to the wants of the general of an army or the humblest traveller. The military, seeing that due regard is paid to their comfort, meet the civil authorities with cordiality, and sternly repress all freebooting and oppression. And as a natural consequence, land near the line of march, instead of being thrown out of cultivation as formerly, is daily rising in value, and the traffic which used to be a curse to the country has become a source of emolument.

And this reminds us of that unequalled Grand Trunk Road along which the commerce of the country rolls, as yet without a tax, in one continued stream. England has her immortal Macadam, but all that he did for English roads was to throw down well-sorted stone fragments, which it was left to the traffic to drive into a close binding soil. Now, in Upper India we have no binding soil and no granite. But by elaborating the limestone of the country (or whatever else kunkur may be), by pounding it up with water and by much beating, a road is made, with great labour and expense, but smooth as a bowling-green. We wish that the patriots of Manchester, who complain of the bad roads of India, would come to see our chief lines of communication in the north-west. We could point with satisfaction to the merchant of Agra bringing his mountains of cotton along a road metalled into one masonry-like embankment, his property guarded by day and watched by night by the servants of Government,* and, except at the

* As a proof of the care taken of travellers, we may remark, that a correspondence lately came under our observation, in which the zealous superintendent of road police complained bitterly to a district magistrate that *gratuitous* police watchmen were not provided for the night guard of all native travellers encamping along the line of the Grand Trunk Road.

The arrangements for watching the Grand Trunk Road in the district with which we happen to be best acquainted are as follows :—Every two miles along the road there is a police station with three policemen. These men are drafted from the body of the district police, are well armed, and wear a becoming uniform. The hours of their respective night-watches are fixed, and each man, on joining a road police-station, has a written notice given him, specifying the precise duties of his post. From 10 p. m. to 4 a. m. two of the three night-guards patrol the road. Horse-patrol are stationed at convenient distances, and to keep them on the alert, a written and verbal parole is sent from the magistrate's court to each end of his district every night. The written parole is returned by the district post, so that the authorities have proof that once, at all events, each night, the horsemen patrol their portion of road. To keep all up to their work, along the forty miles of road three mounted jemadars are stationed, who send in written reports every morning of the exact spot where they passed each horse or foot-patrol during the night. In the district to which we allude, in addition to the

pontoon, or boat-bridges over the Jumna and Ganges, free from all tax or toll. It would be at once conceded to us that, at all events, in the north-western provinces of India trade is less

forty miles of Grand Trunk Road, there is at least an equal length of Branch Trunk Road leading towards Agra, which is watched and patrolled in the same manner. During the past year, no one single case of highway robbery has taken place; and though the traffic has been great, the amount of property stolen at night from travellers at halting-places, so far as can be ascertained, does not exceed twelve hundred rupees (nine hundred of which are the value of a bale of silk cut off a cart under the nose of a sleepy watchman). When it is considered that in this district there are no restraints put upon travellers as to where they shall halt, and that parties of wearied merchants are spending the night all along the road under the canopy of heaven; when the following table of traffic, too, is taken into account, it will be acknowledged that due care is taken to protect the commerce of the country.

Of loaded carts (of one to eight bullocks each) there were 28,168, drawn by 99,714 bullocks. The beasts of burden —camels, bullocks, horses, &c.—carrying loads amounted to 34,820. This is the account of what passed on the Grand Trunk Road alone in the year 1851. Above, *i.e.* to the west of the point where the Agra Branch Road meets the Great Trunk Road, from and to Agra along the branch road, an almost equal amount of traffic passed.

Now, allowing that each bullock and beast of burden drew or carried on an average property worth ten rupees, the losses of merchants by theft in the two roads cannot be set down at more than ten pie per hundred rupees, and by robbery *nil*. And as no single instance of cattle theft occurred during the year on the road, either of loaded or not loaded cattle, the ten pie per hundred rupees must be reduced to at least three pie per hundred rupees, or four pence per hundred pounds sterling.

taxed and better protected than in any other country under the sun.*

So far we have followed the steps of the magistrate, as head of the local police, through the course of his duties both to the public and to the Government under which he serves. A few words may now be spared to the detail of his every-day life. One characteristic marks it,—hard work both for mind and body, but for the mind especially. Were it not for the variety of the distractions which make up his day, it would be impossible for the magistrate to support the amount of wear and tear to which he is exposed.

* The truth is, that in the Agra Presidency men of commerce and capital are cherished and cared for to an undue extent. The merchant princes of Upper India, thanks to our settled Government, excellent bridges, roads, and vigilant police, enjoy advantages which their forefathers never even dreamed of. We grudge them not their wealth and prosperity, nor would we see the Government relax for one moment in its efforts to open out the resources of the country. But we confess, that we should gladly see the commercial classes share with the agricultural population the direct burdens of the State. The progress and stability of our Government have alike opened out new sources of revenue, and we can see no reason why those who profit most from a strong and settled Government should directly share no part of its expenses. The landed communities in general care far less about the security of person and property, which a good system of police has effected, than the commercial classes. The complaint of the landholder is not that he has to pay so much, but that he is called to contribute so exclusively to the State. That statesman will deserve well of India and of England who will summon courage to make all who benefit by British rule contribute equally to its support.

The early morning sees the up-country magistrate riding or walking, far or near, to examine some road or other public work in progress, to visit some disputed tenement, or, failing these objects, to inspect his gaol or prison-factories. On the road, he is beset by people, who, notwithstanding the many hours daily spent by him in cutcherry, vow that they have been unable to obtain a fair hearing. On his return home, a heap of police reports which the district dâk has brought in is waiting; and the public post comes in, too, with its own budget of demands for statements, explanations, and so forth. The police diaries being read and disposed of, with their list of crime, native visitors begin to send in their names before the morning meal is over. It is time to go to cutcherry, but three or four applicants for an interview remain unsatisfied. One word only they have to say, but when once they find themselves inside the house, the one word swells into a long story. At length the magistrate makes a rush to the door, but there he meets a tehsildar from a distant post with returns which require immediate attention. After some half-hour of examination, the tehsildar is dismissed, and once again our functionary, already half fagged, sets off for cutcherry. At his gate, a police report is thrown into his carriage, from a glance at which and at a dead body stretched on a litter, and carried by four villagers, he finds it necessary to go at once to the civil surgeon to ask for details of a *post mortem* examination, which must be made without delay. He is already late for cutcherry, and when he gets there has to pass through a long line of impatient suitors. It takes an hour to receive, read, and explain the orders passed on the petitions thrust upon him by the people. Then comes the regular work of the day. The list of criminals under trial, of witnesses in attendance, of cases ready for orders, is produced; letters to the commissioner of police, the inspectors of prisons, are written, and the day is wearing on, when the head man of the Revenue-office makes his appearance, and produces a goodly bundle of papers. The magistrate asks whether the parties interested in these cases are in attendance, and is answered in the affirmative. The papers are ordered to be brought forward. It is the rule to keep no man waiting; but before the suitors and their witnesses have been collected the head gaoler brings his books; after him comes the stampkeeper, then the man who prepares the road-making accounts, each with a pressing request for one moment's attention, and to them succeeds the record-keeper. The rule is, as we have said, to detain, if possible, no witnesses or people over the day; so that the magistrate finds it nearly dusk before he gets home, weary and worn out. He takes his ride or drive round the same road, and sees the same people that he has seen for the last nine months, eats his dinner, tries to get through an article in the "Quarterly," or a more than usually tempting official printed report. If he goes into society, he is too tired to enjoy it, and wishes himself in bed. Such is the every-day life of the magistrate.

The morning of one day only in the week greets the worn official with some hope of leisure and repose. The magistrate thanks God for Sunday, though the week-day din and rattle of business is still in his ears, and he cannot help to contrast unfavourably an Indian with an English Sunday. In spite of himself, recollections will come up of the merry church-peal, the rural scene dotted with honest villagers hastening up gladly to the house of God,—in short, of all the loved sounds and sights of a Sunday at home. Still he has rest, and is thankful. Beyond this sacred day no real holiday does he know; for though all other business may be brought to an occasional stand, crime takes no rest; and some, indeed, of the magistrate's most anxious days are those of festival and rejoicing to all around him.

We cannot conclude these Notes without a word to the members of the civil service in India. To you we address ourselves, whether young or old, whether high in rank or only entering upon public life, because you can best give effect to any suggestions for the improvement of the people. Few men appreciate the circumstances in which you are placed. Vulgar opinion may still attach the idea of wealth and money-getting to a writership in India, but the delusion is fast wearing away. The days have gone by when the orchestras of Calcutta or Madras used to salute the toast of "the Civil Service" with the popular air of "Money in both pockets." Such a greeting nowadays would be accepted as rather a smart piece of irony, so far is anything like pecuniary affluence from distinguishing your service. Indeed, whilst we could count on our fingers the men whose pockets could jingle responsively to the old-fashioned tune, we might try in vain to enumerate the civil servants who are struggling against the difficulties of impecuniosity. So much the more shame for the service! some may say. But the truth rather is, that, considering what is expected of a man in office, the young civilian—nay, the middle-aged civilian, is but moderately paid. It read very well when Jacquemont wrote to his friends in Paris, how Lord William Bentinck administered the empire of the East with all the simplicity of William Penn. But if a Governor-general can afford to go about like a Quaker, it does not follow that a young assistant to a magistrate may rightly adopt an equal contempt of appearances. He can hardly trudge on foot to cutcherry whilst his subordinate officers have their decent conveyances, nor can the native officials put down their palanquins or ponies so long as the suitors who throng about them travel in good style.

No: it is not money that flings a charm round civil power in India in these days. Even the most able servants of Government, who have grown grey in the study of local laws, manners, and languages, who have worn out a life in heaping up knowledge, for which, beyond the limits of their own presidencies, there is neither use nor demand,—even these men are not better paid than their fellow-men of equal talent and application at home.* But, none the less, there is much to reconcile a generous mind to the sore labours and privations which wait upon civil life in India. Power, a shade, a pretence, a slavery, in England, is a reality here. The power of doing good, not to one or two persons or parishes, but to thousands, is what every civil servant may justly aspire to. The power of mitigating the ills of life, of smoothing its inequalities by lessening injustice, by putting down tyranny, and by encouraging honest exertion,—all this lies in the civilian's daily path. All round the world, in every other country, English statesmen debate, deliberate, argue, or protest; in India alone they seem still privileged to act.

To action, then, we invite every man charged with civil power. Once again we remind you that a noble field lies open to your exertions. Other hands have performed the work of destruction, and have wiped away the ancient empires and monarchies of the East. These have fallen, unpitied, because stained with innocent blood and polluted by injustice. To you belongs the double work of restoration and reform, not by a blind introduction of the law or policy of England, but by grafting English honour and justice upon the institutions of the East.

The work of conquest has been completed, the work of regeneration must begin. Let our soldiers

* The civil servant labours under this disadvantage, that his professional knowledge is useless to him out of India. The soldier, the divine, the surgeon, can find employment at home, but the civilian cannot.

wear, as they have boldly won, the laurels of victory; for the statesmen of India a glorious oaken crown remains. To raise up a degraded race, to cure the plagues of past bad government and bad morals, to prepare—if you may be so blessed—the way for real virtue and true religion,—to this you are called; and look round the world as you may, you will never find a more glorious vocation.